The Quotable Angel

The Quotable Angel

A Treasury of Inspiring Quotations Spanning the Ages

Edited by

LEE ANN CHEARNEY

An Amaranth Book

John Wiley & Sons, Inc.
New York • Chichester • Brisbane • Toronto • Singapore

For Mike,
with love

The editor thanks the following people, angels all, for their assistance and encouragement in the preparation of this book: Linda Ayres-DeMasi, Melanie Belkin, Gene Brissie, Will Camp (for Dante), Diane Chambers, John Cook, Colleen Clifford Corrice, Chris Jackson, Deirdre Kidder, Judith McCarthy, Christine McGoldrick, Andrea Edwards Myers, and, most of all, Bruce Sherwin. Their help is deeply appreciated.

Contents

III. *Angels Infuse Our Perception*

IV. *In Praise of the Sacred*

Foreword

As a child, I was afraid of the dark. Lying in bed at night, barely breathing or moving, the only thing between me and my secret, unspoken fears was my guardian angel. For I believed that I had one. I had no clear picture of my angel. He stood in shadow, mute and brooding, a figure without a name or face, taller than my parents, winged, and always there. Reassured, I would fall asleep and dream not of my angel, but of myself, with wings, surveying the familiar landscape of my childhood:

> Each night in astral dreams, I flew above
> the peaked and pointed spires and steeples
> of the whitewashed town, the streets like spokes
> on a wheel, converging at the circle's center,
> flew over the enthroned moon, fat and full
> as a pumpkin, trying in vain to touch
> its shifting, shimmering surface that rippled
> and flowed like the nightshirts of sleepers
> caught in the crosswinds of a dream. Below,
> the townspeople pointed speechlessly upward
> at a girl flying with outstretched arms
> away from everything she knew. Believe
> or disbelieve a story different from your own.
> I was a chameleon, a dissembler, a conjuror of form . . .
>
> *(Puella Aeterna)*

My dream and the subsequent poem I made out of it spoke of weightlessness, freedom, power and transformation—and the heart's desire of all of us, not just children, to possess the qualities of angels. I dreamed the dream many times over, and then the dream changed and darkened when I was ten or twelve. I was frustratingly earth-bound, no longer able to fly. A landscape "appareled in celestial light" was gone. Wordsworth in his famous ode on childhood was right.

Later, in my adult life, I met my angel face to face. It was soon before I was to leave on sabbatical to spend a year in England. In my dream, I was standing in a church. Light streamed through the high windows, struck and illuminated "my" angel, ageless, perfect, and beautiful. I saw his face, was given his name. The difficult part to describe is not the scene but the emotional tenor of the dream (emotions in dreams always seem purer, clearer, more intense—not mixed and muddied the way they are in waking life). The feeling between us was one of wordless accord, of perfect love. It was a dream of two souls touching. It was, most surely, an annunciation that boded well for the year ahead.

If guardian angels exist, then mine has saved me, in a very literal sense, on several occasions. Talk like this almost always elicits raised eyebrows from skeptical friends. One argues, "But if there are such things as guardian angels, where are they when a child is in an accident, when a child dies?" A belief in angels doesn't mean we are catapulted back into the walled safety of Eden. It simply means a belief in the *possibility*, not certainty, of grace or rescue. For how can we live without such a hope? Without a belief in a pure and boundless energy—love, grace, redemption, call it what you will—that acts as a countervailing force to the world's darkness? Is it preferable to believe that the physical world is all that we have and that the only thing standing between us and oblivion is our own small force and will?

The poet's desire, it might be said, is to write like an angel. To forever fix in language some of the ineffable qualities angels possess. Imagination, for the poet, and the imagination's subsequent embodiment in words, occupies the place that faith and angels occupy for the believer. Imagination for Wallace Stevens was "the necessary angel." Randall Jarrell speaks of the poet standing out in a field, hoping to be struck by lightning six or seven times during a lifetime, surely similar to the epiphanal experiences of saints. The divine moment, for the poet, for the saint or pilgrim, is always the intersection of two worlds: one visible, one invisible, one worldly, one otherworldly, one shadowed, one lightstruck. The poet or artist cannot escape time but his or her creation can—in words, stone, pigment. And so language becomes eternal and the poet occupies the odd and godly position of creator.

We seldom think about the limitations of the angelic lifestyle—what angels selflessly give up in service to the world: the utter lack of a personal life, the first cup of coffee in the morning, meals served in courses with good wine and shining silverware, freshly washed and ironed clothes thoughtlessly put on each morning and just as easily taken off each night, soft beds to sleep in. Angels do not garden, take walks, read books, or paint pictures. (Music seems to be the only diversion angels and humankind share.) Childless and undistracted, angels look to us for their meaning and purpose, waiting to be called upon with the patience of . . . angels.

One can, I suppose, live without angels just as one can live without ever reading a poem, looking at a painting, or listening to a symphony. But such an existence is an impoverishment. The fact of the matter is that, on the deepest level, we *need* angels. Angels (except for a few faulty defective ones) are our own best selves. As mirrors to our own unrealized potentiality and divinity, they speak to the deeper unvoiced parts of our soul and psyche. *The Quotable Angel* takes us back to an earlier time in our lives when belief was everything as it offers up rare and memorable glimpses of the angelic presences among us.

—Elizabeth Spires

Notes from the Editor

*A*ngels are everywhere. Crossing barriers of time, culture, language, religion, and geography, angels infuse the thoughts, dreams, and hopes of all humankind. Guiding stars in the heavens, shepherding the seasons, ministering to the strengths and the frailties of humanity assigned to their care, angels are the divine caretakers of our experience, our world, and our universe. In performing the research for this volume, I was moved by the eloquence of the words people used to talk about angels and by our global need to give voice to the divine—whether to worship, praise, explain, condemn, overcome, or simply to understand.

I eagerly invite the reader to share in this celebration of angels, a celebration as well of the divinity of language and our resolute human striving toward absolute beauty. The words of our world's greatest voices through the centuries—Socrates, Aquinas, da Vinci, Teresa of Avila, Shakespeare, Mozart, Lincoln, Whitman, Einstein, Picasso, Martin Luther King, Jr., Helen Keller, and hundreds of others, spoken as a prayer into the listening ears of our angels, form a chorus that will provoke, inspire, delight, and transport us. Together, we make a celestial pilgrimage to explore the nature of angels, and in doing so we come to discover all that we are,—ourselves, and would hope to be.

The Quotable Angel is divided into four parts: "Our Angels, Ourselves;" "About Angels and Their Mission;" "Angels Infuse Our Perception;" and "In Praise of the Sacred." Each part contains sections that describe a new aspect of angels and our relationship to them. Individual quotations within sections are arranged to guide readers through a progression of speakers and ideas that create resonances and build meaningfully one upon the next. The biographical index and general index can be used to look up quotations by specific speakers or to locate passages by subject. References in quotations that appear gender biased, using the masculine to denote general human nature and angel nature, are the words of the speakers. Readers are encouraged, in such cases, to apply to their understanding of the quotations the spirit of a contemporary sensitivity in regard to the language of gender equality.

Who are angels? How do they look and what do they do? What is there that is angelic in our own human natures? Can it be that the laws of physics are the handiwork of angels? Do angel guardians protect, comfort, and nurture each individual human being? What if there are no angels, but only humankind? *Can* humanity give voice to the divine? Should we try?

We are insatiable in pursuit of a glimpse of the holy. We are filled, as Dante writes in the *Paradiso*, with "an agonizing need of knowing more."

—Lee Ann Chearney

I

*O*ur *A*ngels, Ourselves

Believing in Angels

They say miracles are past, and we have our philosophical
persons, to make modern and familiar, things supernatural
and causeless. Hence it is that we make trifles of terrors,
ensconcing ourselves into seeming knowledge, when we should
submit ourselves to an unknown fear.

WILLIAM SHAKESPEARE
ALL'S WELL THAT ENDS WELL

I believe in angels; angels in heaven, on earth, and in the midmost
air; angels with flaming swords expelling our parents from Paradise
and obstructing Balaam's ass; French angels assisting the Allied
armies at Mons and turning back General Von Kluck's march on
Paris; Ulster angels crowding about Derry; Thomist angels crowding
on needles; weeping angels distressed at what they see; guardian or
tutelary angels steering our wayward course.

ROSE MACAULEY
"BELIEVING" FROM PERSONAL PLEASURES

There is not enough love and kindness in the world to permit us to
give any of it away to imaginary beings.

FRIEDRICH NIETZSCHE
"RELIGIOUS LIFE"

3

The idea that nothing is true except what we comprehend is silly.

WINSTON CHURCHILL

Not only do 96% believe in God, most Americans also believe in: Heaven, 90%; Miracles 79%; Angels, 72%.

USA TODAY/CNN/GALLUP POLL

Make friends with the angels.

ST. AUGUSTINE

So many learned heads should so far forget their metaphysics, and destroy the ladder and scale of creatures, as to question the existence of spirits.

SIR THOMAS BROWNE
RELIGIO MEDICI

A large part of the popularity and persuasiveness of psychology comes from its being a sublimated spiritualism: a secular, ostensibly scientific way of affirming the primacy of "spirit" over matter.

SUSAN SONTAG
ILLNESS AS METAPHOR

The Bible ought to teach him that he will become a black angel and go home to a black God at death.

MARCUS GARVEY
PHILOSOPHY AND OPINIONS OF MARCUS GARVEY

I am convinced that these heavenly beings exist and that they provide unseen aid on our behalf. I do not believe in angels because someone has told me about a dramatic visitation from an angel, impressive as such rare testimonies may be. I do not believe in angels because UFOs are astonishingly angel-like in some of their reported appearances. I do not believe in angels because ESP experts are making the realm of the spirit world seem more and more plausible. I do not believe in angels because of the sudden worldwide emphasis on the reality of Satan and demons. I do not believe in angels because I have ever seen one—because I haven't.

I believe in angels because the Bible says there are angels; and I believe the Bible to be the true Word of God.

I also believe in angels because I have sensed their presence in my life on special occasions.

BILLY GRAHAM
ANGELS: GOD'S SECRET MESSENGERS

*P*robable impossibilities are to be preferred to improbable possibilities.

ARISTOTLE
POETICS

*M*an is certainly stark mad; he cannot make a flea, and yet he will be making gods by dozens.

MICHEL DE MONTAIGNE

*M*aybe they need to conform to our ideas in order to be, in order to exist. Maybe our believing in them and conceiving of them gives [angels] existence.

RICKIE LEE JONES

*I*t seemed to me I was going up to heaven through birchwoods, snow and clouds of smoke, with all those plump women, those bearded peasants tirelessly making their signs of the cross.

MARC CHAGALL
MY LIFE

*S*o long as man remains free he strives for nothing so incessantly and so painfully as to find someone to worship.

FEDOR DOSTOEVSKY
THE BROTHERS KARAMAZOV

*T*here is no question that there is an unseen world. The problem is, how far is it from midtown and how late is it open? Unexplainable events occur constantly. One man will see spirits. Another will hear voices. A third will wake up and find himself running in the Preakness.

WOODY ALLEN
"EXAMINING PSYCHIC PHENOMENA"

*W*e must be linked up with the Holy Angels: we must form with them one strong family.

POPE PIUS XII

*B*ut the Angel came only to Mary, and no one could understand her. After all, what woman was so mortified as Mary? And is it not true in this instance also that one whom God blesses he curses in the same breath?

SOREN KIERKEGAARD
FEAR AND TREMBLING

[Mary] was so full of grace, so pure, so full of God. She looked at the angel—she must have been surprised for she had never seen an angel—and asked, how? What are you saying? I don't understand what you are saying; it makes no sense to me. And the angel said simply that by the power of the Holy Spirit, Christ would be formed within her. And Mary answered simply, "Behold the handmaid of the Lord."

MOTHER TERESA
TOTAL SURRENDER

. . . the angel Gabriel was sent from God unto a city of Galilee, named Nazareth, to a virgin espoused to a man whose name was Joseph, of the house of David; and the virgin's name was Mary. And the angel came in unto her, and said, Hail, thou that art highly favoured, the Lord is with thee: blessed art thou among women. And when she saw him, she was troubled at this saying, and cast in her mind what manner of salutation this should be. And the angel said unto her, Fear not, Mary: for thou has found favour with God. And, behold, thou shalt conceive in thy womb, and bring forth a son, and shalt call his name JESUS. He shall be great, and shall be called the Son of the Highest: and the Lord God shall give unto him the throne of his father David: And he shall reign over the house of Jacob for ever; and of his kingdom there shall be no end.

LUKE 1:26–33

To believe in something not yet proved and to underwrite it with our lives; it is the only way we can leave the future open.

LILLIAN SMITH
THE JOURNEY

What one heart finds hard to believe, a hundred find easy.

NANCY WILLARD
THINGS INVISIBLE TO SEE

*I*t is convenient that there be gods, and, as it is convenient, let us believe there are.

OVID

*A*nd they know neither sect nor idolatry, with the exception that all believe that the source of all power and goodness is in the sky, and they believe very firmly that I, with these ships and people, came from the sky, and in this belief they everywhere received me, after they had overcome their fear.

CHRISTOPHER COLUMBUS

*O*ne does not become enlightened by imagining figures of light, but by making the darkness conscious.

C. G. JUNG

Peter Pan: Do you believe in fairies? Say quick that you believe! If you believe, clap your hands!

J. M. BARRIE

*W*e believe as much as we can. We would believe everything if we could.

WILLIAM JAMES

"*H*aving cleared away blind faith, we no longer have any spiritual burdens.

MAO TSE-TUNG

"Angels don't exist. They are an error of semantics," Miguel would argue.

"Don't be a heretic, Miguel."

"They were just ordinary messengers until St. Thomas Aquinas came up with all that humbug."

"Do you mean to tell me that the feather of the Archangel Saint Gabriel they venerate in Rome was plucked from the tail of a buzzard?" laughed Gilberto.

"If you don't believe in angels you don't believe in anything. You should be in a different profession," Filomena chimed in.

"Several centuries have been lost arguing how many of those creatures can dance on the head of a pin. Who cares? A man shouldn't waste his energy on angels, he should help people!"

ISABEL ALLENDE
"A DISCREET MIRACLE"

If you don't believe in the gods, leave them alone.

CHINESE PROVERB

Songs of
the Angels

And now it is an angel's song
That makes the heavens be mute.

SAMUEL TAYLOR COLERIDGE
"THE RIME OF THE ANCIENT MARINER"

The spirit will not descend without song.

AFRICAN PROVERB

Whether the angels play only Bach in praising God I am not quite sure; I am sure, however, that *en famille* they play Mozart.

KARL BARTH

If there is whistling in the great beyond, I'll kill myself.

JEAN STAFFORD
THE CATHERINE WHEEL

It is the song of the angels sung by earth spirits.

E. H. W. MEYERSTEIN
ON BEETHOVEN'S NINTH SYMPHONY

I looked up at the clouds, and two men were coming there, head-first like arrows slanting down; and they came, they sang a sacred song and the thunder was like drumming. I will sing it for you. The song and the drumming were like this: "Behold, a sacred voice is calling you; All over the sky a sacred voice is calling."

BLACK ELK

*S*he was our angel, the sweet angel of sex, and the sugar of sex came up from her like a resonance of sound in the clearest grain of a violin.

NORMAN MAILER
MARILYN

*T*he secret of creation lay in music. "A *voice* to light gave being." Sound led the stars to their places.

LYDIA MARIA CHILD
LETTERS FROM NEW YORK

*S*well the vast song till it mounts to the sky!
  Angels of Bethlehem, echo the strain!

OLIVER WENDELL HOLMES
"HYMN OF PEACE"

*I*t came upon a midnight clear,
That glorious song of old,
From Angels bending near the earth
To touch their harps of gold:
"Peace on the earth; good will to man
From Heaven's all gracious King."
The world in solemn stillness lay
To hear the angels sing.

EDMUND HAMILTON SEARS

*G*abriel blow de trumpet horn,
Hallelujah!

AFRICAN-AMERICAN SPIRITUAL

*S*o from the lights that there to me appeared
  Upgathered through the cross a melody,
  Which rapt me, not distinguishing the hymn.

DANTE ALIGHIERI
PARADISO, CANTO XIV

*A*deste fideles, Laeti triumphantes, Venite, Venite, in Bethlehem.
Natum videte, Regem angelorum, Venite adoramus, Venite adoramus,
Venite adoramus, Dominum.

JOHN FRANCIS WADE

Angels we have heard on high
Sweetly singing o'er the plains,
And the mountains in reply,
Echoing their joyous strains.
Gloria in excelsis Deo.

19TH-CENTURY HYMN

Hark! the herald angels sing

CHARLES WESLEY
"CHRISTMAS HYMN"

Singing singing is singing is singing is singing is singing between
between singing is singing is between singing is.

GERTRUDE STEIN

She is screaming   singing hymns   her thin human wings
          spread out
From her neat shoulders   the air beast-crooning to her   warbling

JAMES DICKEY
"FALLING"

Angel lute   also, angelica (It.), angelique (Fr.), angelot   a fretted
two-necked lute of the late 17th and 18th c. similar to the theorbo,
with two sets of strings situated side-by-side rather than in courses,
and tuned diatonically.

PHILIP D. MOREHEAD
THE NEW INTERNATIONAL DICTIONARY OF MUSIC

At this point I told Harpo I didn't want to hear any more horns.

He honked.

I said, "Say it with strings."

So he grabbed his harp and proceeded to play me to sleep. I snored in accompaniment.

GROUCHO MARX

Angels
Within Us

*B*elieve there is a great power silently working all things for good, behave yourself and never mind the rest.

BEATRIX POTTER

I have been on the verge of being an angel all my life, but it's never happened yet.

MARK TWAIN

*P*oets are damned but they are not blind, they see with the eyes of the angels.

WILLIAM CARLOS WILLIAMS
INTRODUCTION TO ALLEN GINSBERG'S HOWL

*T*he uninhabited angel! That is what you have always been hunting!

DJUNA BARNES
NIGHTWOOD

$\mathcal{A}$ man does not have to be an angel in order to be a saint.

ALBERT SCHWEITZER

$\mathcal{W}$hen I'm good, I'm very good, but when I'm bad I'm better.

MAE WEST
IN I'M NO ANGEL

$\mathcal{T}$o embody the transcendent is why we are here.

SOGYAL RINPOCHE
TIBETAN BOOK OF LIVING AND DYING

$\mathcal{A}$ngels are pointing . . . to what we call God, but not this righteous, jealous, watchful deity. But rather, a source of energy which is even more unfathomably loving than the angel. And this ocean of love is us, and we come from it and we go back to it, and all the cells of our bodies are composed of it.

SOPHY BURNHAM
A BOOK OF ANGELS

$\mathcal{T}$o transmute a man into an angel was the hope that drove him all over the world and never let him flinch from a meeting or withhold goodbyes for long. This hope insistently divided his life into only two parts, journey and rest.

EUDORA WELTY
"A STILL MOMENT"

$\mathcal{W}$e can never really know. I simply believe that some part of the human Self or Soul is not subject to the laws of space and time.

C. G. JUNG

*T*he pure joy angels feel is like fresh air for the soul. Like a sky-light opening, the angel within you can illuminate any circumstance and see everything in a perfect natural light once more. The angel within us is our most basic soul, unfettered.

KAREN GOLDMAN

. . . *A*nd whatsoever you see of spiritual forms and
of things visible whose countenance is godly to
behold and whatsoever you see of thought,
imagination, intelligence, soul and the heart with
its Secret and whatsoever you see of Angelic aspect,
or things whereof Satan is the spirit . . .
Lo, I, the Perfect Man, am that whole, and
that whole is my theatre . . .
The sensible world is mine, and the Angel-world
is of my weaving and fashioning.

ABDUL KARIM JILI

*A*ct for God, if you want to—be *God's* actress, if you want to. What could be prettier?

J. D. SALINGER
FRANNY AND ZOEY

*M*aybe the tragedy of the human race was that we had forgotten we were each Divine.

SHIRLEY MACLAINE
OUT ON A LIMB

*I*s birth always a fall?
Do angels have wings? Can men fly?

SALMAN RUSHDIE

*O*ne tries to cure the signs of growth, to exorcise them, as if they were devils, when really they might be angels of annunciation.

Angels of annunciation of what? Of a new stage in living when, having shed many of the physical struggles, the worldly ambitions, the material encumbrances of active life, one might be free to fulfill the neglected side of one's self. One might be free for growth of mind, heart, and talent; free at last for spiritual growth; free of the clamping sunrise shell.

ANNE MORROW LINDBERGH
GIFT FROM THE SEA

*T*here's a very nice feeling that there are many, many spirits inside of me looking after me, along with my own sort of nuclei spirit.

WHOOPI GOLDBERG

*E*veryone entrusted with a mission is an angel . . . All forces that reside in the body are angels.

MAIMONIDES

*A*rt thou some god, some angel, or some devil?

WILLIAM SHAKESPEARE
JULIUS CAESAR

*N*ever give up on anybody. Miracles happen every day.

H. JACKSON BROWN, JR.
LIFE'S LITTLE INSTRUCTION BOOK

*I*nfinite worlds appear and disappear in the vast expanse of my own consciousness, like motes of dust dancing in a beam of light.

ANCIENT VEDIC SAYING

*N*o matter what we talk about, we are talking about ourselves.

HUGH PRATHER
I TOUCH THE EARTH, THE EARTH TOUCHES ME

*T*here are moments in our lives, there are moments in a day, when we seem to see beyond the usual—become clairvoyant.

ROBERT HENRI

All we have to remember is this: Seeing holiness only in others—or only in our own group—is the problem. Seeing the sacred in ourselves and in all living things is the solution.

GLORIA STEINEM
REVOLUTION FROM WITHIN

*A*ngelic Soul

[*A*ngels] guide us to become spiritual people for the pleasure of it, not for its moralism, because the spiritual life itself has a great deal of beauty and real satisfaction, even pleasure. And this is what the soul needs.

THOMAS MOORE

*R*ather than a soul in a body, become a body in a soul.

GARY ZUKAV
THOUGHTS FROM THE SEAT OF THE SOUL

*D*o you imagine that Byron could have written his powerful poems in the midst of turmoil, or that Dante was surrounded by distractions while his soul was journeying amongst the shades? Without the soul there is no continuity, nothing creative. Work is constantly interrupted, and it all comes from associating with too many people.

EUGENE DELACROIX
IN A JOURNAL ENTRY, MAY 18, 1824

The soul should always stand ajar, ready to welcome the ecstatic experience.

EMILY DICKINSON

I began to think of the soul as if it were a castle made of a single diamond or of very clear crystal, in where there are many rooms, just as in Heaven there are many mansions.

ST. TERESA OF AVILA

If I have freedom in my love,
And in my soul am free;
Angels alone, that soar above,
Enjoy such liberty.

RICHARD LOVELACE
"TO ALTHEA, FROM PRISON"

It is only with the heart that one can see rightly; what is essential is invisible to the eye.

ANTOINE DE SAINT-EXUPERY
THE LITTLE PRINCE

. . . And I am imagining how it would be if we could infuse souls.

VIRGINIA WOOLF

The value of a man is not in his skin, that we should touch him.

HENRY DAVID THOREAU
SOLITUDE

*A*nd neither the angels in Heaven above
Nor the demons down under the sea,
Can ever dissever my soul from the soul
Of the beautiful Annabel Lee.

EDGAR ALLAN POE
"ANNABEL LEE"

*D*reams and feelings survive with the endurance of the eternal,
Universal Soul, though they might wane at times and subside at
others, just as does the sun with the approach of night or the moon
with the advent of the morn.

KAHLIL GIBRAN
SPIRIT BRIDES

*A*nd the more souls who resonate together,
   the greater the intensity of their love,
      and, mirror-like, each soul reflects the other.

DANTE ALIGHIERI

*W*hy, if the Soul can fling the Dust aside,
And naked on the Air of Heaven ride,
   Were't not a Shame—were't not a Shame for him
In this clay carcase crippled to abide?

RUBAIYAT OF OMAR KHAYYAM

I feel myself a soul as immense as the world, truly a soul as deep as
the deepest rivers, my chest has the power to expand without limit. I
am a master and I am advised to adopt the humility of the cripple.
Yesterday, awakening to the world, I saw the sky turn upon itself
utterly and wholly. I wanted to rise, but the disemboweled silence

fell back upon me, its wings paralyzed. Without responsibility, strad-
dling Nothingness and Infinity, I began to weep.

FRANTZ FANON
BLACK SKIN, WHITE MASKS

The soul is kissed by God in its innermost regions.

HILDEGARDE OF BINGEN

Color is the keyboard, the eyes are the hammers, the soul is the
piano with many strings. The artist is the hand which plays, touching
one key or another, to cause vibrations in the soul.

WASSILY KANDINSKY
CONCERNING THE SPIRITUAL IN ART

And you O my soul where you stand,
Surrounded, detached, in measureless oceans of space,
Ceaselessly musing, venturing, throwing, seeking the spheres
        to connect them,
Till the bridge you will need be form'd, till the ductile
        anchor hold,
Till the gossamer thread you fling catch somewhere, O my
        soul.

WALT WHITMAN
"A NOISELESS PATIENT SPIDER"

I was thrown out of college for cheating on the metaphysics exam; I
looked into the soul of the boy next to me.

WOODY ALLEN

Angel Visions

In the beginning God created the heaven and the earth. And the earth was without form and void; and darkness was upon the face of the deep. And the Spirit of God moved upon the face of the waters.

GENESIS 1:1–2

In thoughts of the visions of the night, I saw long rows of angels in paradise, each with his hands in a jar of spermaceti.

HERMAN MELVILLE
MOBY DICK

I have never seen angels. Show me an angel and I will paint one.

GUSTAV COURBET
ON A REQUEST TO PAINT A CHURCH MURAL, 1850

Maybe other angels have dropped into other Elm Street back-yards? Behind fences, did neighbors help earlier hurt ones? Folks keep so much of the best stuff quiet, don't they.

ALLAN GURGANUS
"IT HAD WINGS"

Oh, their Rafael of the dear Madonnas,
Oh, their Dante of the dread Inferno,
Wrote one song—and in my brain I sing it,
Drew one angel—borne, see, on my bosom!

ROBERT BROWNING
"ONE WORD MORE"

Let brotherly love continue. Be not forgetful to entertain strangers
for thereby some have entertained angels unawares.

HEBREWS 13:1–2

If angels are entertained unaware, it is because they have tact.

SPENCER BAYNE
"MURDER RECALLS VAN KILL"

The Angel of God, upon the threshold seated,
Which seemed to me a stone of diamond.

DANTE ALIGHIERI
PURGATORIO, CANTO IX

'Tis only when they spring to heaven that angels
Reveal themselves to you.

ROBERT BROWNING
PARACELSUS, PART V

For without being seen, [angels] are present around us.

ST. FRANCIS DE SALES

*A*nd, behold, there was a great earthquake: for the angel of the Lord descended from heaven, and came and rolled back the stone from the door, and sat upon it. His countenance was like lightning, and his raiment white as snow: And for fear of him the keepers did shake, and became as dead men. And the angel answered and said unto the women, Fear not ye: for I know that ye seek Jesus, which was crucified. This is not here: for he is risen, as he said.

MATTHEW 28:2–6

*E*verything appears to us in the guise of "figures."

PABLO PICASSO

*C*omic Angels: And Other Approaches to Greek Drama Through Vase-Painting

OLIVER TAPLIN
BOOK TITLE

*I*n scripture the visitation of an angel is always alarming; it has to begin by saying "Fear not." The Victorian angel looks as if it were going to say, "There, there."

C. S. LEWIS
THE SCREWTAPE LETTERS

I state right from the outset: "Be not afraid!" . . . *Christ addressed this invitation many times to those He met.* The angel said to Mary: "Be not afraid!" The same was said to Joseph: "Be not afraid!" Christ said the same to the apostles, to Peter, in various circumstances, and especially after His Resurrection. He kept telling them: "Be not afraid!" He sensed, in fact, that they were afraid. They were not sure if who they saw was the same Christ they had known. They were afraid when He was arrested; they were even more afraid after his Resurrection.

The words Christ uttered are repeated by the Church. *And with the Church, they are repeated by the Pope.* I have done so since the first homily I gave in St. Peter's Square: "Be not afraid!" These are not words said into a void. They are profoundly rooted in the Gospel. They are simply the words of Christ Himself.

POPE JOHN PAUL II
CROSSING THE THRESHOLD OF HOPE

Angels and ministers of grace defend us!
Be thou a spirit of health, or goblin damn'd,
Bring with thee airs from heaven, or blasts from hell,
Be thy intents wicked, or charitable,
Thou com'st in such a questionable shape
That I will speak to thee.

WILLIAM SHAKESPEARE
HAMLET

The passage from Revelations sent a frisson of accustomed delight
through the frame of Mrs. Papagay . . . all its strange visions and
images, the angels rolling up the scroll of the heavens and tidying
them away forever, the stars falling out of the sky into the sea like a
rain of golden fiery globes, the dragons and swords, the blood and
the honey, the swarms of locusts and the hosts of angels, those creatures at once pure white and fiery-eyed, casting down their golden
crowns around a glassy sea.

A. S. BYATT
THE CONJUGIAL ANGEL

Then, suddenly and dramatically, the dull routine was shattered by
the appearance of an angel.

BILLY GRAHAM
"CHRISTMAS ANGELS"

Abishag my angel has risen from her chair and approaches without
noise, wearing only a vivid scarf. Her eyes are dark as the tents of
Kedar. I want my God back; and they send me a girl.

JOSEPH HELLER
GOD KNOWS

God says: If you come to My House, I will come to yours.

HILLEL

The fireplace was an old one, built by some Dutch merchant long ago, and paved all round with quaint Dutch tiles, designed to illustrate the Scriptures. There were Cains and Abels, Pharaohs' daughters, Queens of Sheba, Angelic messengers descending through the air on clouds like feather-beds, Abrahams, Belshazzars, Apostles putting off to sea in butter-boats, hundreds of figures to distract his thoughts; and yet the face of Marley, seven years dead, came like the ancient Prophet's rod, and swallowed up the whole. If each smooth tile had been a blank at first, with power to shape some picture on its surface from the disjointed fragments of his thoughts, there would have been a copy of old Marley's head on every one.

CHARLES DICKENS
A CHRISTMAS CAROL

Now and then when the room was otherwise lightless a misty grey figure would appear to be seated on this bench in the alcove. It was the tender and melancholy figure of an angel or some dim, elderly madonna. The apparition occurred in the alcove most often on those winter nights in New Orleans when slow rain is falling from a sky not clouded heavily enough to altogether separate the town from the moon.

TENNESSEE WILLIAMS
"THE ANGEL IN THE ALCOVE"

And David lifted up his eyes and saw the angel of the Lord stand between the earth and the heaven, having a drawn sword in his hand stretched out over Jerusalem.

I CHRONICLES 21:16

Thus in the bosom of a cloud of flowers
   Which from those hands angelical ascended,
   And downward fell again inside and out,
Over her snow-white veil with olive cinct
   Appeared a lady under a green mantle,
   Vested in color of the living flame

DANTE ALIGHIERI
PURGATORIO, CANTO XXX

ON THE GROUP OF THE THREE ANGELS
BEFORE THE TENT OF ABRAHAM, BY RAFFAELLE, IN THE VATICAN

*O*h, now I feel as though another sense
From Heaven descending had inform'd my soul;
I feel the pleasurable, full control
Of Grace, harmonious, boundless, and intense.
In thee, Celestial Group, embodied lives
The subtle mystery; that speaking gives
Itself resolv'd: the essences combin'd
Of Motion ceaseless, Unity complete.
Borne like a leaf by some soft eddying wind,
Mine eyes, impell'd as by enchantment sweet,
From part to part with circling motion rove,
Yet seem unconscious of the power to move;
From line to line through endless changes run,
O'er countless shapes, yet seem to gaze on One.

WASHINGTON ALLSTON

*B*lessed are the pure in heart: for they shall see God.

MATTHEW 5:8

*A*ngels of
*M*ercy

I think that wherever your journey takes you, there are new gods waiting there, with divine patience—and laughter.

SUSAN M. WATKINS

*A*ngel of Peace, thou has wandered too long!
  Spread thy white wings to the sunshine of love!

OLIVER WENDELL HOLMES
"HYMN OF PEACE"

*W*e shall find peace. We shall hear the angels, we shall see the sky sparkling with diamonds.

ANTON CHEKHOV
UNCLE VANYA

O welcome pure-eyed Faith, white-handed Hope,
Thou hovering angel girt with golden wings.

JOHN MILTON

*T*ake what the gods give while their hands are open, for none know what they will withhold when they are shut.

AFRICAN PROVERB

*I*f you refuse this offer, you will be the most ungrateful, wicked girl and the angels will weep for you.

REX HARRISON
AS HENRY HIGGINS IN GEORGE CUKOR'S MY FAIR LADY,
ON OFFERING ELIZA DOOLITTLE SPEECH LESSONS

I heard an Angel singing,
When the day was springing,
"Mercy, Pity, Peace
Is the world's release."

WILLIAM BLAKE

*M*other Teresa tells a story of walking past an open drain and catching a glimpse of something moving in it. She investigated and found a dying man whom she took back to a home where he could die in love and peace.

"I live like an animal in the streets," the man told her. "Now I will die like an angel."

MOTHER TERESA
WORDS TO LIVE BY . . .

*I*s it likely God, with angels singing round him,
       Hears our weeping any more?

ELIZABETH BARRETT BROWNING

... *A*nd the Lord sent an angel of mercy who annointed her head with a polo mallet and of the ten plagues, the Lord sent one through six, inclusive, and Job was sore and his wife angry and she rent her garment and then raised the rent but refused to paint.

WOODY ALLEN
"THE SCROLLS"

*T*hen cherish pity, lest you drive an angel from your door.

WILLIAM BLAKE
"HOLY THURSDAY"

*G*race fills empty spaces, but it can only enter where there is a void to receive it, and it is grace itself which makes this void.

SIMONE WEIL

*W*hom but a dusk misfeatured messenger,
No other than the angel of this life,
Whose care is lest men see too much at once.

ROBERT BROWNING
THE RING AND THE BOOK

Healing Powers of Angels

*A*re they not ministering spirits, sent forth to minister for them who shall be heirs of salvation?

HEBREWS 1:14

A ministering angel shall my sister be.

WILLIAM SHAKESPEARE
HAMLET

*A*ngels are the great strangers in this time. It is necessary to speak much more about them as ministers of providence in the government of the world and of men.

POPE JOHN PAUL I
(THE POPE OF 30 DAYS)

*Y*ou know, Michael, I bet it would make a great series about an angel coming back and helping out.

LYNN LANDON
TO MICHAEL LANDON AS THE INSPIRATION FOR HIGHWAY TO HEAVEN

*A*ngels represent God's personal care for each one of us.

FR. ANDREW GREELEY

*A*ngels want us to be whole, as God is whole. Angels are whole beings without hurts or wounds in them, [and] they want that for us very much. And so they work with us in whatever ways they can to help us heal our lives. Not usually by doing the work for us, but by showing us what we need to do, and supporting us with extra love, wisdom, encouragement, and peace.

EILEEN ELIAS FREEMAN

*O*h sovereign angel,
Wide winged stranger above a forgetful earth,
Care for me, care for me. Keep me unaware of danger
And not regretful
And not forgetful of my innocent birth.

EDNA ST. VINCENT MILLAY

*S*o ending flows to beginning
like the cry of a swan.
We are in a sickroom.
But the night belongs to the angels.

NELLY SACHS
"IN THE EVENING YOUR VISION WIDENS"

*A*ngel: You know me Prophet: Your battered heart,
Bleeding Life in the Universe of Wounds.

TONY KUSHNER
ANGELS IN AMERICA, PART II

I know that my work in this case is magnified by the fact that the streets of heaven are too crowded with angels. We know their names. They number a thousand for each one of the red ribbons that we wear here tonight. They finally rest, in the warm embrace of the gracious creator of us all. A healing embrace that cools their fevers, that clears their skin, and allows their eyes to see the simple, self-evident, commonsense truth that is made manifest by the benevolent creator of us all and was written down on paper by wise men, tolerant men, in the city of Philadelphia two hundred years ago. God bless you all. God have mercy on us all, and God bless America.

TOM HANKS
ACCEPTING THE ACADEMY AWARD
FOR BEST ACTOR, 1993

I cannot find a substitute word for all that is most holy but I have tried to deflect people's attention into offering to each other what they offer to an Unseen Being in the sky. When people are holy to each other, war will end, human suffering will end.

BESSIE HEAD

*A*nd yet, when I look up to the sky, I somehow feel that everything will change for the better, that this cruelty too shall end, that peace and tranquility will return once more.

ANNE FRANK

$\mathcal{N}$or is it in an Angel's godlike power
To lengthen out [life's] wasting thread one single hour.

THOMAS COLE
"THE VOYAGE OF LIFE, PART SECOND"

$\mathcal{W}$hen my daughter Veronica died 16 years ago, I believe she became an angel. It was then that I started painting angels and haven't been able to stop.

MAUREEN GAFFNEY-WOLFSON

$\mathcal{B}$esides, the few miracles attributed to the angel showed a certain mental disorder, like the blind man who didn't recover his sight but grew three new teeth, or the paralytic who didn't get to walk but almost won the lottery, and the leper whose sores sprouted sunflowers. Those consolation miracles, which were more like mocking fun, had already ruined the angel's reputation when the woman who had been changed into a spider finally crushed him completely.

GABRIEL GARCIA MARQUEZ
"A VERY OLD MAN WITH ENORMOUS WINGS"

$\mathcal{A}$nd is there enough magic out there in the moonlight to make this dream come true?

BURT LANCASTER
AS DOC "MOONLIGHT" GRAHAM IN PHIL ALDEN ROBINSON'S FIELD OF DREAMS

$\mathcal{H}$ealed of my hurt, I laud the inhuman Sea—
Yea, bless the Angels Four that there convene;
For healed I am even by their pitiless breath
Distilled in wholesome dew named rosmarine.

HERMAN MELVILLE
PEBBLES

Sometimes I go about in pity for myself,
    and all the while
A great wind is bearing me across the sky.

OJIBWA CHANT

Even though you cannot see this guardian tangibly, when you feel longing, compulsion, or pain you know that there is such a thing as a guardian. For example, you feel the softness of the underwater flowers and plants; but when you go to the farther side you are scratched by thorns. So you know—even though you see neither one—that the farther side is where thorns grow, a place of unpleas-antness and pain, whereas this side is where flowers grow, a place of comfort.

JALALUDDIN RUMI
SIGNS OF THE UNSEEN

A black Jew and an angel to boot—very hard to believe, but sup-pose he had been sent to succor him, and he, Manischevitz, was in his blindness too blind to comprehend? It was this thought that put him on the knife-point of agony.

BERNARD MALAMUD
"ANGEL LEVINE"

Miracles . . . seem to me to rest not so much upon faces or voices or healing power coming suddenly near to us from afar off, but upon our perceptions being made finer, so that for a moment our eyes can see and our ears can hear what is there about us always.

WILLA CATHER
DEATH COMES FOR THE ARCHBISHOP

And when he came to the den, he cried with a lamentable voice unto Daniel: and the king spake and said to Daniel, O Daniel, servant of the living God, is thy God, whom thou servest continually, able to deliver thee from the lions? Then said Daniel unto the king, O king, live for ever. My God hath sent his angel, and hath shut the lions' mouths, that they have not hurt me: forasmuch as before him innocency was found in me; and also before thee, O king, have I done no hurt.

DANIEL 6:20-22

Angels to Watch Over Us

*A*ll night, all day, angels watchin' over me, my Lord. All night, all day, angels watchin' over me.

AFRICAN-AMERICAN SPIRITUAL

*A*ngellike protection [is] offered to everyone, even those who don't want us looking after them.

CURTIS SLIWA

*S*ee, I am sending an angel ahead of you to guard you along the way . . .

EXODUS 23:2

*S*he took to telling the truth; she said she was forty-two and five months. It may have been pleasing to the angels, but her elder sister was not gratified.

SAKI (H. H. MUNRO)

*G*od committed the care of men and all things under heaven to Angels.

JUSTIN MARTYR

*C*oming, clutching each other with old, invented
forms of grace and clumsy gratitude, ready
to be alone again, or dissatisfied, or merely
companionable like the couples on the summer beach
reading magazine articles about intimacy between the sexes
to themselves, and to each other,
and to the immense, illiterate, consoling angels.

ROBERT HASS
"PRIVILEGE OF BEING"

*B*ut men must know, that in this theater of man's life it is reserved
only for God and the angels to be lookers on.

FRANCIS BACON
ADVANCEMENT OF LEARNING

*T*o marry is to domesticate the Recording Angel. Once you are
married, there is nothing left for you, not even suicide, but to be
good.

ROBERT LOUIS STEVENSON

*T*here are two angels that attend unseen
Each one of us, and in great books record
Our good and evil deeds

HENRY WADSWORTH LONGFELLOW

A pretty woman as was ever seen,
Fresh as the Angel o'er a new inn door.

LORD BYRON
BEPPO

*A*nd I never felt more a part of the remote and overpressing world, or more full of love and arrogance and pity and humility, not for myself alone, but for the living earth I suffered on and for the unfeeling systems in the upper air, Mars and Venus and Brazell and Skully, men in China and St. Thomas, scorning girls and ready girls, soldiers and bullies and policemen and sharp, suspicious buyers of second-hand books, bad ragged women who'd pretend against the museum wall for a cup of tea, and perfect, unapproachable women out of fashion magazines, seven feet high, sailing slowly in their flat, glazed creations through steel and glass and velvet.

DYLAN THOMAS
PORTRAIT OF THE ARTIST AS A YOUNG DOG

*B*etween angels, on this earth
absurdly between angels, I
try to navigate

STEPHEN DUNN
"BETWEEN ANGELS"

*D*id the star-wheels and angel wings, with
their holy winnowings,
Keep beside you all the way?

ELIZABETH BARRETT BROWNING

*S*ome people are aware of everything that is going on everywhere at every moment in their lives.

ANNE TYLER
CELESTIAL NAVIGATION

*A*las, a mortal may not lean
On Heaven, when Heaven averts its mien.

VIRGIL
THE AENEID

*H*is is alone; but still deserted never
The Angel yet shall watch is perilous way,
And though the clouds of earth may seem to sever,
Still through the darkness shines the Angelic ray;
And in the hour of midnight o'er the deep
The Guardian Spirit kind will constant vigil keep.

THOMAS COLE

*G*od has a TV set and God watches us on it. Whenever I think I'm being watched, I always sing and dance and do a commerical for myself.

JANE WAGNER
EDITH ANNE, MY LIFE, SO FAR

*T*hey went to sleep then. Michelangelo, Angel, and the entire Italian Renaissance waited for them until morning.

E. L. KONIGSBERG
FROM THE MIXED-UP FILES OF MRS. BASIL E. FRANKWEILER

The spiritual is real and permeates all existence so that the ancestral spirits, the living dead, are all around us, concerned to promote the well-being of those who are bound together with them in the bundle of life. They are the guardians of morality to ensure the essential harmony of the community remains intact. And so before you partake of a drink you spill a little as a libation to acknowledge the presence of this ever present cloud of witnesses surrounding the living and yet to be born.

DESMOND TUTU
THE AFRICAN PRAYER BOOK

There is one God looking down on us all. We are all children of one God. God is listening to me. The sun, the darkness, the winds, are all listening to what we now say.

GERONIMO

As on the bridge, with half-closed eyes
and mouths about to speak, the twelve
    Bernini angels, in their cold
        and heavy robes,

    and wings unfurled with the weight of men,
were in alignment yet reluctant to pass
    from this to the next sleep.
        And who would know—

        and what would they tell us?

STANLEY PLUMLY
"MEN WORKING ON WINGS"

*D*uring all this time the angels (with one exception; God had probably had trouble with this one before) merely looked on and watched—the serene and blameless seraphim, that white and shining congeries who, with the exception of that one whose arrogance and pride God had already had to curb, were content merely to bask for eternity in the reflected glory of the miracle of man, content merely to watch, uninvolved and not even caring, while man ran his worthless and unregretted course toward and at last into that twilight where he would be no more. Because they were white, immaculate, negative, without past, without thought or grief or regrets or hopes, except that one—the splendid dark incorrigible one, who possessed the arrogance and pride to demand with, and the temerity to object with, and the ambition to substitute with—

WILLIAM FAULKNER
ADDRESS TO THE GRADUATING CLASS OF PINE MANOR JUNIOR COLLEGE

II

About Angels and Their Mission

Angel Guides

We are like children, who stand in need of masters to enlighten us and direct us; and God has provided for this, by appointing his angels to be our teachers and guides.

ST. THOMAS AQUINAS

Behold, I send an Angel before thee, to keep thee in the way, and to bring thee into the place which I have prepared.

EXODUS 23:20

Lighthouses are more helpful than churches.

BENJAMIN FRANKLIN

You should be rul'd and led
By some discretion that discerns your state
Better then you yourself.

WILLIAM SHAKESPEARE
KING LEAR

*A*nd naught prevented men from believing when the guidance came to them but that they said, "Has God sent forth a mortal as messenger? Say: "Had here been in the earth angels walking at peace, We would have sent down upon them out of heaven an angel as messenger."

THE KORAN

*P*assing beyond the teaching of the Angels, the soul goes on to the knowledge and understanding of things, no longer merely betrothed but dwelling with the bridegroom.

CLEMENT OF ALEXANDRIA

*F*or an angel of peace, a faithful guide, a guardian of our souls and bodies, let us entreat the Lord.

LITURGY OF THE EASTERN ORTHODOX CHURCH

*T*ell me my heart,—what angel-greeted door

DANTE GABRIEL ROSSETTI

*F*or he shall give his angels charge over thee: to keep thee in all
    thy ways
They shall bear thee in their hands: that thou hurt not thy foot
    against a stone.

BOOK OF COMMON PRAYER

*Y*es, I companion him to places
    Only dreamers know.

THOMAS HARDY

*L*ean on me and follow me; when the abysses gape below, close your eyes. Trust my step and the high, icy spirit. Then we two shall be like God.

PAUL KLEE

*B*ut what exactly was a "guiding spirit?" What were these spirit guides that I encountered almost everywhere, forbidding one thing, commanding another to be done? I could not understand it at all, though their presences surrounded me as I grew to manhood. There were good spirits, and there were evil ones; and more evil ones than good ones, it seemed.

CAMARA LAYE
THE DARK CHILD

*M*ichael row de boat ashore,
Hallelujah!

AFRICAN-AMERICAN SPIRITUAL

I believe we are free, within limits, and yet there is an unseen hand, a guiding angel, that somehow, like a submerged propeller, drives us on.

RABINDRANATH TAGORE

*Y*ea, whiles I was speaking in prayer, even the man Gabriel whom I had seen in the vision at the beginning, being caused to fly swiftly, touched me about the time of the evening oblation. And he informed me, and talked with me, and said, O Daniel, I am now come forth to give thee skill and understanding.

DANIEL 9:21-22

*U*pon the stern sat the Celestial Pilot;
    Beatitude seemed written in his face,
    And more than a hundred spirits sat within.

DANTE ALIGHIERI
PURGATORIO, CANTO II

*A*nd the captain of the Lord's host said unto Joshua, Loose thy shoe from off thy foot; for the place whereon thou standest is holy. And Joshua did so.

JOSHUA 5:15

Angels to Intercede

For fools rush in where angels fear to tread.

ALEXANDER POPE
ESSAY ON CRITICISM

Angels rush in when fools is almost dead.

RUDOLPH FISHER
BLADES OF STEEL

Then if angels fight,
Weak men must fall, for heaven still guards the right.

WILLIAM SHAKESPEARE
RICHARD II

I do the very best I know how—the very best I can; and I mean to keep doing so until the end. If the end brings me out all right, what is said against me won't amount to anything. If the end brings me out wrong, ten angels swearing I was right would make no difference.

ABRAHAM LINCOLN

I do believe that the buck stops here, that I cannot rely upon public opinion polls to tell me what is right. I do believe that right makes might and that if I am wrong, ten angels swearing I was right would make no difference. I do believe, with all my heart and mind and spirit, that I, not as President, but as a humble servant of God, will receive justice without mercy if I fail to show mercy.

GERALD R. FORD
ANNOUNCING HIS DECISION TO PARDON FORMER U.S. PRESIDENT RICHARD M. NIXON,
SEPTEMBER 8, 1974

I'm certain that if we are to solve the problems on earth, we will have to do it ourselves. New Age theology says we live in a benign universe where all you have to do is ask an angel for help. This makes things like Sarajevo difficult to understand.

TONY KUSHNER

*G*od does not deal directly with man; it is by means of spirits that all the intercourse and communication of gods with men, both in waking life and in sleep, is carried on.

SOCRATES

*M*y woman asked the girl if she believed the book were written under the influence of Divine Power, if she considered the book to be a religious text of some sort.

The girl said, "No."

RICHARD BRAUTIGAN
TROUT FISHING IN AMERICA

*T*rue friendship is a knot that angel hands have tied.

ANONYMOUS

*I*n quibbles angel and archangel join,
And God the Father turns a school-divine.

ALEXANDER POPE
ON MILTON'S PARADISE LOST

*T*he air was filled with phantoms, wandering hither and thither in
restless haste, and moaning as they went. . . . Many had been per-
sonally known to Scrooge in their lives. He had been quite familiar
with one old ghost, in a white waistcoat, with a monstrous iron safe
attached to its ankle, who cried piteously at being unable to assist a
wretched woman with an infant, whom it saw below, upon a door-
step. The misery with them all was, clearly, that they sought to inter-
fere, for good, in human matters, and had lost the power for ever.

CHARLES DICKENS
A CHRISTMAS CAROL

*F*or . . . Christ is the King's Attorney;
Who pleads for all without degrees,
And he hath angels, but no fees;

SIR WALTER RALEIGH
"THE PILGRIMAGE"

*S*ynchronicities seem to occur when we need them most.

JAMES REDFIELD AND CAROL ADRIENNE
THE CELESTINE PROPHECY: AN EXPERIENTIAL GUIDE

*S*he felt again that small shiver that occurred to her when events
hinted at a destiny being played out, of unseen forces intervening.

DOROTHY GILMAN

First Voice: But why drives on that ship so fast,
Without or wave or wind?

*The Mariner hath been cast into a trance; for the angelic power causeth
the vessel to drive northward faster than human life could endure.*

SAMUEL TAYLOR COLERIDGE
"THE RIME OF THE ANCIENT MARINER"

$\mathcal{M}$any people purchase property insurance, health insurance, and car insurance. They do not want to be stranded in times of unforeseen misfortune. Why not an Angel Insurance Policy rooted in Angel Power? Angel Power is a free gift of God available to everyone. An Angel Insurance Policy will give you a blessed hedge against the unforeseen.

JANICE T. CONNELL
ANGEL POWER

$\mathcal{H}$ow oft do they their silver bowers leave,
　　To come to succour us that succour want!
　　How oft do they with goldon pinions cleave
　　The flitting skyes, like flying pursuivant,
　　Against fowle feendes to ayd us militant!
　　They for us fight, they watch, and dewly ward,
　　And their bright squadrons round about us plant;
　　And all for love, and nothing for reward;
O, why should heavenly God to men have such regard!

EDMUND SPENSER
"THE MINISTRY OF ANGELS!"

$\mathcal{A}$nd when we cried unto the Lord, he heard our voice, and sent an angel, and hath brought us forth out of Egypt.

NUMBERS 20:16

$\mathcal{A}$nd, behold, the angel of the Lord came upon him, and a light shined in the prison: and he smote Peter on the side, and raised him up, saying, Arise up quickly. And his chains fell off from his hands.

ACTS 12:7

*B*ut it is presumption in us when
The help of heaven we count the act of men.

WILLIAM SHAKESPEARE
ALL'S WELL THAT ENDS WELL

A vision of a young woman came back to me, a memory of a beautiful and energetic spirit who had once been waiting to come to
earth. I remembered her as the young spirit with whom I shared a
bond in a previous time, the one in the spirit world whose loveliness
and energy captivated me. I wanted to cry as everything about this
precious angel came together.

BETTY J. EADIE
EMBRACED BY THE LIGHT

Angels by Name

Not Angles but Angels.

POPE GREGORY I (THE GREAT)

And the angel of the Lord said unto him, Why asketh thou thus after my name, seeing it is secret?

JUDGES 13:18

Angels and archangels may have gathered there,
Cherubim and seraphim thronged the air;
But his mother only, in her maiden bliss,
Worshipped the beloved with a kiss.

CHRISTINA ROSSETTI
"IN THE BLEAK MID-WINTER"

SERAPHINS ET SERAPHINES

Bands on zebras, Hordes on quaggas. Like a field of tulips in March wind. Argot Porcupine Minor.

GUY DAVENPORT
"APPLES AND PEARS"

WINTER

*T*hus said the Lord in the Vault above the Cherubim
Calling to the Angels and the Souls in their degree.

RUDYARD KIPLING
"THE LAST CHANTEY"

*H*ear all ye angels, progeny of light,
Thrones, dominations, princedoms, virtues, powers.

JOHN MILTON
PARADISE LOST

. . . *T*he seraph Abdiel, faithful found
Among the faithless, faithful only he;
Among innumerable false, unmoved,
Unshaken, unseduced, unterrified,
His loyalty he kept, his love, his zeal;
Nor number, nor example with him wrought
To swerve from truth, or change his constant mind,
Though single. From amidst them forth he passed,
Long way through hostile scorn, which he sustained
Superior, nor of violence feared aught;
And with retorted scorn his back he turned
On those proud towers to swift destruction doomed.

JOHN MILTON
"ABDIEL" FROM PARADISE LOST

. . . *H*e gathers the prayers as he stands,
And they change into flowers in his hands,
Into garlands of purple and red.

HENRY WADSWORTH LONGFELLOW
"SANDALPHON"

*A*ngela Greek: "heavenly messenger." Var. and dim: Angel,
Angele, Angelina, Angeline, Angelita, Angie, Angy.

A TREASURY OF BABY NAMES

*Y*es, Heaven is thine; but this
        Is a world of sweets and sours;
        Our flowers are merely—flowers,
And the shadow of thy perfect bliss
        Is the sunshine of ours.

If I could dwell
Where Israfel
        Hath dwelt, and he where I,
He might not sing so wildly well
        A mortal melody,
While a bolder note than this might swell
        From my lyre within the sky.

EDGAR ALLAN POE
"ISRAFEL"

I am the Angel of the Sun
Whose flaming wheels began to run
When God's almighty breath
Said to the darkness and the Night,
Let there be light! And there was light
I bring the gift of Faith.

HENRY WADSWORTH LONGFELLOW
"RAPHAEL" FROM THE NATIVITY

*T*he three Divine are in this hierarchy,
  First the Dominions, and the Virtues next;
  And the third order is that of the Powers.
Then in the dances twain penultimate
  The Principalities and Archangels wheel;
  The last is wholly of angelic sports.
These orders upward all of them are gazing,
  And downward so prevail, that unto God
  They all attracted are and all attract.

DANTE ALIGHIERI
PARADISO, CANTO XXVIII

The Angel, four divine emanations, Fluor, Phosphor, Lumen and Candle; manifest in One: the Continental Principality of America. She has magnificent gray steel wings.

TONY KUSHNER
ANGELS IN AMERICA, PART II

*N*ay—*peace be still—*
lovest thou not Azrael,

the last and greatest, Death?
lovest not the sun,

the first who giveth life,
Raphael? *lovest thou me?*

lover of sand and shell,
know who withdraws the veil,

holds back the tide and shapes
shells to the wave-shapes? Gabriel:

Raphael, Gabriel, Azrael,
three of seven—what is War

to Birth, to Change, to Death?
yet he, red-fire is one of seven fires,

judgement and will of God
God's very breath—Uriel.

H. D.
"TRIBUTE TO THE ANGELS"

*O*ne could go further and claim that *all* of the angels mentioned in the Bible by name—Michael, Gabriel, Raphael, and Uriel—are meant to represent God in His immanence.

FRANK J. TIPLER
THE PHYSICS OF IMMORTALITY

A sad self-knowledge, withering, fell
On the beauty of Uriel.

RALPH WALDO EMERSON
"URIEL"

*A*nd the angel of the Lord appeared unto him in a flame of fire out
of the midst of a bush: and he looked, and, behold, the bush burned
with fire, and the bush was not consumed. And Moses said, I will
now turn aside, and see this great sight, why the bush is not burnt.
And when the Lord saw that he turned aside to see, God called unto
him out of the midst of the bush, and said, Moses, Moses. And he
said, Here *am* I. . . . And Moses said unto God, Behold, *when* I come
unto the children of Israel, and shall say unto them, The God of
your fathers hath sent me unto you; and they shall say to me, What
is his name? what shall I say unto them? And God said unto Moses, I
AM THAT I AM: and he said, Thus shalt thou say unto the children
of Israel, I AM hath sent me unto you.

EXODUS 3:2–4, 13-14

$\mathcal{A}$ngelic
$\mathcal{L}$ove

$\mathcal{A}$ll that I am, or hope to be, I owe to my angel mother.

ABRAHAM LINCOLN
IN A REMARK TO HIS LAW PARTNER, WILLIAM HERNDON

$\mathcal{A}$ human being is a part of the whole, called by us "the universe." Our task must be to widen our circle of compassion to embrace all living creatures and the whole of nature in its beauty.

ALBERT EINSTEIN

$\mathcal{T}$his is the right way of approaching or being initiated into the mysteries of love, to begin with examples of beauty in this world, and using them as steps to ascend continually with that absolute beauty as one's aim, from one instance of physical beauty to two and from two to all, then from physical beauty to moral beauty, and from moral beauty to the beauty of knowledge, until from knowledge of various kinds one arrives at the supreme knowledge whose sole object is that absolute beauty, and knows at last what absolute beauty is.

PLATO
SYMPOSIUM

67

*B*eauty is unbearable, drives us to despair, offering us for a minute the glimpse of an eternity that we should like to stretch out over the whole of time.

ALBERT CAMUS

*S*WAK: Sealed With Angel Kisses

ANONYMOUS

*J*oin in on the movement and go out and do a random act of kindness. Then say, "My angel made me do it."

SALLY SHARP

I didn't see any wing on his shoulder, you understand? But I [will] tell you something . . . there must be something, a bigger power who asked him to do the job. And to find yourself on Schindler's list, you find yourself on the list of life.

LEOPOLD PAGE
HOLOCAUST SURVIVOR

*D*ear George:
  Remember *no* man is a failure who has friends.
    Thanks for the wings!
Love,
  Clarence

FRANK CAPRA
IT'S A WONDERFUL LIFE

*T*hough I speak with the tongues of men and of angels, and have not charity, I am become as sounding brass, or a tinkling cymbal.

I CORINTHIANS 13:1

*L*ove's heralds should be thoughts . . .
Therefore do nimble-pinioned doves draw love,
And therefore hath the wind-swift Cupid wings.

WILLIAM SHAKESPEARE
ROMEO AND JULIET

*L*ove, your beauty is not a mortal thing:
there is no face among us that can equal
the image in the heart, which you kindle and sustain
with another fire and stir with other wings.

MICHELANGELO BUONARROTI

*T*hen as an angel, face and wings
Of air, not pure as it, yet pure doth wear,
    So thy love may be my love's sphere.
        Just such disparity.
As is 'twixt air and angels' purity,
'Twixt women's love and men's will ever be.

JOHN DONNE
"AIR AND ANGELS"

O Lyric Love, half angel and half bird,
And all a wonder and a wild desire.

ROBERT BROWNING

A perfect woman, nobly planned,
To warn, to comfort, and command;
And yet a Spirit still, and bright
With something of angelic light.

WILLIAM WORDSWORTH
"SHE WAS A PHANTOM OF DELIGHT"

'*T*is strange what a man may do, and a woman yet think him an angel.

WILLIAM MAKEPEACE THACKERAY
THE HISTORY OF HENRY ESMOND

*W*omen are angels, wooing:
Things won are done; joy's soul lies in the doing.

WILLIAM SHAKESPEARE
TROILUS AND CRESSIDA

*S*he is haunted by visions of an Angel, and her passion for him amounts to obsession; to her he is Good, and no one else she meets is of any significance, except as help in her search for the Angel, or his physical embodiment, Heinrich.

KOBBE'S OPERA BOOK
ON L'ANGE DE FEU BY SERGEI PROKOFIEV

Sir Frederic: And if I don't find Angel?

Lady Maria/Angel: In that case, I think you'll want to see your lawyer as soon as possible. On the other hand, if you don't go in at all, you will be a little uncertain. You won't be so sure of yourself—or of me. And that might be wonderful.

MARLENE DIETRICH
AS LADY MARIA/ANGEL IN ANGEL

*S*he loves not you nor me as we all love her.
Yea, though we sang as angels in her ear,
        She would not hear.

ALGERNON CHARLES SWINBURNE

*E*very lover is a warrior, and Cupid has his camps.

OVID

*L*ove looks not with the eyes, but with the mind,
And therefore is winged Cupid painted blind.

WILLIAM SHAKESPEARE
A MIDSUMMER NIGHT'S DREAM

" 'The angels keep their ancient places; Turn but a stone, and start a wing! 'Tis ye, 'tis ye, your estranged faces, that miss the many-splendored thing.' "

As he was speaking Gavin's eyes had not left her face. Again, he bent and kissed her full on the mouth.

"I'm so glad that we didn't miss our many-splendored thing, Rosie."

BARBARA TAYLOR BRADFORD
ANGEL

And the angel said, "I have learned that every man lives, not through care of himself, but by love."

LEO TOLSTOY

For I am persuaded, that neither death, nor life, nor angels, nor principalities, nor powers, nor things present, nor things to come. Nor height, nor depth, nor any other creature, shall be able to separate us from the love of God.

ROMANS 8:38

Toy heard the sound of trumpets and suddenly saw legions of angels assembling beneath the big tent, chattering and giggling among themselves. They were dark ones, light ones, small ones, tall ones. Some were children, some were adults. There were no wings or halos, but Toy saw exquisite colors swirling around each being and could feel their overwhelming love.

NANCY TAYLOR ROSENBERG
CALIFORNIA ANGEL

And they provoked in these experts, who had never seen angels in life, but only in art, a yearning to know. It was as if [the angels] held the purest emotion, love, embodied in wood, as if irresistible, transforming love had carved them as close to life as they could come without the holy spark.

ROSANNE DARYL THOMAS
THE ANGEL CARVER

The conclusion is always the same: love is the most powerful and still the most unknown energy of the world.

PIERRE TEILHARD DE CHARDIN

Flight of Angels

*I*t felt as if the angels were pushing.

LIEUTENANT-GENERAL ADOLF GALLAND
ON 1ST FLIGHT IN A JET AIRCRAFT, THE MESSERSCHMITT 262, MAY 1943

*A*ngels can fly because they take themselves lightly.

G. K. CHESTERTON

*I*f you surrendered to the air, you could *ride* it.

TONI MORRISON
SONG OF SOLOMON

*T*here was a shifting of stars, a glimmering of blue light, and he felt himself surrounded by blueness and suspended. A moment later he was deposited, with a gentle bump, upon the rock . . .

RAY BRADBURY
"THE FIRE BALLOONS"

An angel needs no passport.

CARY GRANT
AS DUDLEY IN HENRY KOSTER'S THE BISHOP'S WIFE

The secret of seeing is to sail on solar wind. Hone and spread your spirit, till you yourself are a sail, whetted, translucent, broadside to the merest puff.

ANNIE DILLARD

You are loosened from your moorings, and are free; I am fast in my chains, and am a slave! You move merrily before the gentle gale, and I sadly before the bloody whip! You are freedom's swift-winged angels, that fly around the world; I am confined in bands of iron! O that I were free! O, that I were on one of the gallant decks, and under your protecting wing! Alas! betwixt me and you, the turbid waters roll. Go on, go on. O that I could also go! Could I but swim! If I could fly! O, why was I born a man, of whom to make a brute!

FREDERICK DOUGLASS
ON WATCHING SHIPS SAIL THE CHESAPEAKE

Love wants to be lofty and to be restrained by nothing lowly. . . . He who loves soars, runs and rejoices; he is free and without bonds.

HENRI MATISSE
JAZZ

Soul-forward, headlong

VIRGINIA WOOLF

Gibreel, the tuneless soloist, had been cavorting in moonlight as he sang his impromptu gazal, swimming in air, butterfly-stroke, breast-stroke, bunching himself into a ball, spreadeagling himself against the almost-infinity of the almost-dawn, adopting heraldic postures, rampant, couchant, pitting levity against gravity.

SALMAN RUSHDIE
THE SATANIC VERSES

My soul is awakened, my spirit is soaring
And carried aloft on the wings of the breeze.

ANNE BRONTE

They shout if it can fly call it a flier
The angels flutter around the youthful flutterer

GUILLAUME APOLLINAIRE

We are the stars which sing.
We sing with our light.
We are the birds of fire.
We fly over the sky.
Our light is a voice
We make a road
For the spirit to pass over.

PASSAMAQUODDY CHANT

What angel nightly tracks that waste of frozen snow.

EMILY BRONTE
"THE VISIONARY"

*H*ow like an Angel came I down!

THOMAS TRAHERNE
"WONDER"

I hope you love birds, too. It is economical. It saves going to Heaven.

EMILY DICKINSON

*M*ovement never lies.

MARTHA GRAHAM

I determined to travel with the wind and the stars.

JACQUELINE COCHRAN

*W*ho has seen the wind?
Neither you nor I;
But when the trees bow down their heads,
The wind is passing by.

CHRISTINA ROSSETTI

*E*verything That Rises Must Converge

FLANNERY O'CONNOR
BOOK TITLE

*O*ne can never consent to creep when one feels an impulse to soar.

HELEN KELLER

*C*ourage is the price that life exacts for granting peace.
The soul that knows it not, knows no release
From little things;
Knows not the livid loneliness of fear,
Nor mountain heights where bitter joy can hear
The sound of wings.

AMELIA EARHART

*W*hen I fly, I think about three things: faith, hope, and gravity.

MILTON BERLE

Once, as we dashed onward like a hurricane, there was a flutter of wings and the bright appearance of an angel in the air, speeding forth on some heavenly mission.

NATHANIEL HAWTHORNE
"THE CELESTIAL RAILROAD"

For Christians and Muslims the great mystery is the fall: of human kind, but also of the angels. The great fall of the most beautiful angel, the lieutenant of the heavenly hosts: Lucifer. But Lucifer, as far as we know, is irredeemable; he is doomed for all eternity. Human beings, on the other hand, can pay for their sins, can change the fall into flight.

OCTAVIO PAZ

As they drew close to the glittering, pleated, roaring weir, Carter had the sudden distinct feeling that he should look behind him. And there was the heron, sailing out of the woods toward them, against the wind, held, indeed, motionless within the wind, standing in midair with his six-foot wingspread—an angel.

JOHN UPDIKE
"THE AFTERLIFE"

My kite's skin is fluttering.

NATIVE AMERICAN SAYING

Feel the life-force that floats . . .

VIRGINIA SATIR

O, speak again, bright angel, for thou art
As glorious to this night, being o'er my head,
As is a winged messenger of heaven
Unto the white-upturned wond'ring eyes
Of mortals that fall back to gaze on him,
When he bestrides the lazy puffing clouds,
And sails upon the bosom of the air.

WILLIAM SHAKESPEARE
ROMEO AND JULIET

*H*earing the air cleft by their verdant wings,
  The serpent fled, and round the Angels wheeled,
  Up to their stations flying back alike

DANTE ALIGHIERI
PURGATORIO, CANTO VIII

Wings

*P*hilosophy will clip an angel's wings.

JOHN KEATS

*T*he more materialistic science becomes, the more angels shall I paint: their wings are my protest in favor of the immortality of the soul.

SIR EDWARD COLEY BURNE-JONES
IN A LETTER TO OSCAR WILDE

*H*e heard an odd voice, as though of a whirring . . . and when he strained for a wider view, could have sworn he saw a dark figure born aloft on a pair of strong black wings.

BERNARD MALAMUD
"ANGEL LEVINE"

*T*eacher says every time a bell rings, an angel gets his wings.

KAROLYN GRIMES
AS ZUZU IN FRANK CAPRA'S IT'S A WONDERFUL LIFE

Would that I were under the cliffs, in secret hiding places
     of the rocks,
that Zeus might change me to a winged bird.

EURIPIDES

God sends forth the angels as His messengers with two, three, or
four pairs of wings.

THE KORAN

The function of the wing is to take what is heavy and raise it up in
the region above.

PLATO

An angel whose muscles developed no more power weight for
weight than those of an eagle or a pigeon would require a breast
projecting for about four feet to house the muscles engaged in working its wings, while to economize in weight, its legs would have to be
reduced to mere stilts.

J. B. S. HALDANE

If I seen him bearing down on me now under whitespread wings
like he'd come from Arkangels, I sink I'd die down over his feet,
humbly dumbly, only to washup.

JAMES JOYCE
FINNEGANS WAKE

Winged words.

HOMER
THE ILIAD

All along the white beach, up and down, there was no living thing in sight. A bird with a broken wing was beating the air above, reeling, fluttering, circling disabled down, down to the water.

KATE CHOPIN
THE AWAKENING

So many wings come here
dipping honey
and speak here
in your home Oh
God

AZTEC VERSE

With angel's wings thy soul shall mount
To bliss unseen by eye,
And drink at unexhausted fount
Of joy unto eternity.

ANNE BRADSTREET

Cum, listen w'ile yore Unkel sings
Erbout how low sweet chariot swings,
Truint Angel, wifout wings

RAY GARFIELD DANDRIDGE

Life on earth means: to eat bread and transform the bread into wings, to drink water and transform the water into wings. Life on earth means: the sprouting of wings.

NIKOS KAZANTZAKIS
THE LAST TEMPTATION OF CHRIST

I see spirit-tufts of downy white feathers.

OWL WOMAN

*W*hen I was seventeen and beginning to wonder what I was going to do with my life, I started dreaming about angels. Night after night they would come to me softly, so softly that I could never quite see their faces. But when they turned to go I would see their wings. And in the mornings when I'd sit on the side of my bed staring down at my two long white feet, it was remembering those wings, transparent like a dragonfly's and quivering slightly, that made me start thinking of religion.

APRIL STEVENS
ANGEL, ANGEL

A corner draft fluttered the flame
And the white fever of temptation
Upswept its angel wings that cast
A cruciform shadow.

BORIS PASTERNAK
DOCTOR ZHIVAGO, A POEM BY YURII ZHIVAGO

*A*ll the Utopias will come to pass only when we grow wings and all people are converted into angels.

FEDOR DOSTOEVSKY
"THE DIARY OF A WRITER"

*T*he wind was in their wings.

ZECHARIAH 5:9

*O*h Pray My Wings Are Gonna Fit Me Well

MAYA ANGELOU
BOOK TITLE

Angel Dress and Appearance

We trust in plumed procession
For such the angels go—
Rank after Rank, with even feet—
And uniforms of Snow.

EMILY DICKINSON
"To fight aloud, is very brave"

The garments of the angels correspond to their intelligence. The garments of some glitter as with flame and those of others are resplendent as with light: others are of various colors, and some white and opaque.

The angels of the inmost heaven are naked, because they are in innocence and nakedness corresponds to innocence. It is because garments represent states of wisdom that they are so much spoken of in the Word, in relation to the Church and good men.

EMANUEL SWENDENBORG

Their garments are white, but with an unearthly whiteness. I cannot describe it, because it cannot be compared to earthly whiteness; it is much softer to the eye. These bright Angels are enveloped in a light so different from ours that by comparison everything else seems dark. When you see a band of fifty you are lost in amazement. They seem clothed with golden plates, constantly moving, like so many suns.

PERE LAMY

Veronese: Michelangelo, at Rome, in the Pontifical Chapel, painted our Lord Jesus Christ, His Most Holy Mother, St. John, St. Peter, and the Court of Heaven, all of them naked, from the Virgin Mary down, with little reverence.

Inquisition: Do you not know that in painting the Last Judgment, in which no garments or such things are supposed to be, there was no need of painting clothes, and in those figures there is nothing that is not spiritual, and there are no jesters, dogs, weapons, or such like buffooneries?

VERONESE
DEFENDING HIS PAINTING, SUPPER IN THE HOUSE OF LEVI, 1573

I should have liked to have an angelic brush and heavenly forms for delineating the Archangel, and to see him in Paradise. But I was unable to ascend so high, and I sought him on earth in vain.

GUIDO RENI
ON HIS PAINTING, ST. MICHAEL FIGHTING THE DEVIL

*T*he imagery of dazzling, often blinding, light also symbolizes the spirituality of angels. Pure spirits, totally incorporeal beings, cannot be painted, nor can they be described in words that call images to mind. Only by using the symbolism of light, which makes the invisible visible, can painters and poets try to prevent an egregious misunderstanding of the imagery they are compelled to employ. The bodily forms and features that they depict angels as having must be recognized as pictorial metaphors, not as literal representations of what angels are like.

MORTIMER J. ADLER
THE ANGELS AND US

*F*or it is not the shape, but their use, that makes them angels.

THOMAS HOBBES

*U*nseen as the pure spirits called angels.

POPE PAUL VI

[*T*hese new angels] might not have perfect hair and be the perfect model types. In "Angels 88," you're going to find these girls sometimes wearing no makeup at all. Particularly, you know, when they are running around on the beach.

TONY SHEPHERD
ON ANNOUNCING A NEW SERIES DEVELOPED BY AARON SPELLING PRODUCTIONS

ANGEL: AMIENS CATHEDRAL

O spirit embodied, but without
need of body, made without artifice
by Mind and worked in stone,
what was your Maker thinking of?
Your face smooth and untroubled
as a newborn's, the brow cool
and the eyes blind, one finger
touching the air, most fair of elements.
All is appearance, you tell us,
wearing the weight of stone wings,
stone clothes, without complaining.
Perhaps you, too, once had a flaw—
a thought, no more than that,
less than angelic. In a second
of a second, you were restored
to innocence by a Maker omniscient
and kind. The thought was gone.
But you were someplace other than
heaven. And changed to stone.

ELIZABETH SPIRES

*W*e hear of the arm, hand, finger, and face of God, among other
physical references; and the angels of God, indistinguishable from
God himself, have male bodies including (one can infer) genitalia.
But perhaps because, even in everyday life, human language uses
the parts and functions of the human body in endlessly metaphorical
ways, these anthropomorphisms never seem to derogate in the
slightest from the godlikeness of God.

JACK MILES
GOD: A BIOGRAPHY

I often see through things right to the apparition itself.

GRACE PALEY

$\mathcal{A}$sked whether she felt their warmth when she embraced them, she replied that she could scarcely embrace them without feeling and touching them. They spoke to her in French, addressing her as *Jehanne la Pucelle, fille de Dieu.* Why should they speak English, she asked, when they were not on the English side? They smelt good, and wore beautiful crowns, but she could not, or would not, describe their clothes. Asked whether Saint Michael was naked or not, she retaliated by enquiring scornfully whether they imagined that Our Lord had not the wherewithal to clothe him? . . . Saint Michael had wings, she said, but she would not say anything about the bodies or limbs of Catharine and Margaret. . . . They appeared to her several times a day, especially if she were in a wood. Whenever they came they brought guidance and comfort.

VITA SACKVILLE-WEST
SAINT JOAN OF ARC

$\mathcal{T}$he tragedy of our time is that we are so eye centered, so appearance besotted.

JESSAMYN WEST
LOVE IS NOT WHAT YOU THINK

$\mathcal{A}$ppearances to the mind are of four kinds. Things either are what they appear to be; or they neither are, nor appear to be; or they are, and do not appear to be; or they are not, and yet appear to be.

EPICTETUS

$\mathcal{T}$he equation of appearance and disappearance, the truth of the body and the nonbody, the vision of the presence that dissolves into splendour: pure vitality, a heartbeat of time.

OCTAVIO PAZ

The Indian counterpart of the black Christ is the Christmas card portraying the Holy Family living in a hogan in Monument Valley on the Navaho reservation. As the shepherds sing and gather their flocks, little groups of Navaho angels announce the birth of the Christchild. The scene is totally patronizing and unrealistic.

VINE DELORIA, JR.
WE TALK, YOU LISTEN

There is a coal-black Angel
    With a thick Afric lip

HERMAN MELVILLE

The Ethiopians say that their gods are snub-nosed and black, the Thracians that theirs have light blue eyes and red hair.

XENOPHANES

The Examining Angels in the Koran have blue eyes as the most repulsive of all their features.

ALEXANDER THEROUX
THE PRIMARY COLORS

For some, It was Pure Voice and Radiance and not a figure at all, but for everyone I spoke to or looked at, It was Actuality—and It could be ignored or interpreted as one liked but only at one's peril: that was admitted.

HAROLD BRODKEY
STORIES IN AN ALMOST CLASSICAL MODE

As for the likeness of the living creatures, their appearance was
like burning coals of fire, and like the appearance of lamps: it went
up and down among the living creatures, and the fire was bright,
and out of the fire went forth lightning. And the living creatures ran
and returned as the appearance of a flash of lightning.

EZEKIEL 1:13–14

Their faces had they all of living flame,
    And wings of gold, and all the rest so white
    No snow unto that limit doth attain

DANTE ALIGHIERI
PARADISO, CANTO XXX

On Earth and In Heaven

Are there not angels and men, heaven and earth?

POPE GREGORY I (THE GREAT)

Numerous are the angels in heaven.

THE KORAN

Praise the world to the angel, not the untellable. You cannot impress him with the splendour you have felt; in the cosmos where he feels with greater feeling you are a novice. So show him the simple thing.

RAINER MARIA RILKE

One must rise above the Earth to become universal.

JEAN TOOMER

Saw in the sun a mighty angel stand.

ROBERT BURNS
"THE COTTER'S SATURDAY NIGHT"

*L*ook how the floor of heaven
Is thick inlaid with patens of bright gold.
There's not the smallest orb which thou beholds't
But in his motion like an angel sings,
Still quiring to young ey'd cherubins;
Such harmony is in immortal souls,
But whilst this muddy vesture of decay
Doth grossly close it in, we cannot hear it.

WILLIAM SHAKESPEARE
THE MERCHANT OF VENICE

*H*opes, that were Angels at their birth,
But died when young, like things of earth.

JAMES MONTGOMERY
"NIGHT"

*C*reator of all things visible and invisible, spiritual and corporeal;
who by his almighty power, together at the beginning of time,
formed out of nothing the spiritual creature and the corporeal creature, that is, the angelic and the terrestrial; and then the human
creature, composed of both body and spirit.

FOURTH LATERAN COUNCIL, 1215

"*T*o be" is to inter-be. We cannot just be by ourselves alone. We
have to inter-be with every other thing.

THICH NHAT HANH
PEACE IS EVERY STEP

To be as God, can be understood in two ways; first, by equality;
secondly, by likeness. An angel could not seek to be as God in the
first way, because by natural knowledge he knew that this was
impossible. . . . And even supposing it were possible, it would be

against natural desire, because there exists in everything the natural desire to preserve its own nature which would not be preserved were it to be changed into another nature. Consequently, no creature of a lower nature can ever covet the grade of a higher nature, just as an ass does not desire to be a horse.

ST. THOMAS AQUINAS

*V*ast chain of being! which from God began,
Natures aethereal, human, angel, man,
Beast, bird, fish, insect, what no eye can see,
No glass can reach.

ALEXANDER POPE
"ESSAY ON MAN"

*A*ll is a miracle. The stupendous order of nature, the revolution of a hundred millions of worlds around a million of stars, the activity of light, the life of all animals, all are grand and perpetual miracles.

VOLTAIRE

*A*ngelheaded hipsters burning for the ancient heavenly connection
    to the starry dynamo in the
            machinery of night

ALLEN GINSBERG
HOWL

*H*e raised a mortal to the skies;
She drew an angel down.

JOHN DRYDEN

*T*hou hast the sweetest face I ever look'd on.
Sir, as I have a soul, she is an angel.

WILLIAM SHAKESPEARE
HENRY VIII

I am a little world made cunningly
of elements, and an angelic sprite.

JOHN DONNE

*W*omen would be no more superstitious today than men, if they
had been men's political and business equals and gone outside the
four walls of home and the other four of the church into the great
world, and come in contact with and discussed men and measure on
the plane of this mundane sphere, instead of living in the air with
Jesus and the angels.

SUSAN B. ANTHONY
IN A LETTER TO ELIZABETH CADY STANTON, 1896

*T*he world is not to be put in order, the world is order. It is for us
to put ourselves in unison with this order.

HENRY MILLER

*E*very day is a god, each day is a god, and holiness holds forth
in time.

ANNIE DILLARD

*T*o me every hour of the light and dark is a miracle,
Every cubic inch of space is a miracle.

WALT WHITMAN

*T*he wars among nations on earth are merely popgun affairs compared to the fierceness of the battle in the spiritual unseen world.

BILLY GRAHAM

The angels carry out the arrangements of the universe, that is to say, that though on the surface, stars and the sun and the moon and the elements carry out their functions, yet in reality it is carried out by angels . . . whatever is happening in the physical system does not take place without the mediation of angels.

MIRZA GHULAM AHMAD

Spiritual love is a position of standing with one hand extended into the universe and one hand extended into the world, letting ourselves be a conduit for passing energy.

CHRISTINA BALDWIN

My words fly up, my thoughts remain below:
Words without thoughts never to heaven go.

WILLIAM SHAKESPEARE
HAMLET

We ought not to ask why the human mind troubles to fathom the secrets of the heavens. . . . The diversity of Nature is so great, and the treasures hidden in the heavens so rich, precisely in order that the human mind shall never be lacking in fresh nourishment.

JOHANNES KEPLER
MYSTERIUM COSMOGRAPHICUM

The trees reflected in the river—they are unconscious of a spiritual world so near them. So are we.

NATHANIEL HAWTHORNE
AMERICAN NOTEBOOKS

Angels of Death

Good-night sweet prince,
And flights of angels sing thee to thy rest!

WILLIAM SHAKESPEARE
HAMLET

This was the Angel of History! We felt its wings flutter through the
room. Was that not the future we awaited so anxiously?

JOSEF GOEBBELS
ON HEARING OF THE DEATH OF U.S. PRESIDENT FRANKLIN DELANO ROOSEVELT

Very often, [in near-death experiences] the person encounters a
divine or angelic being. This may be described as Christ, an angel,
even God. Typically [people] don't report these beings as having the
wings we see in the paintings, but rather as luminescent beings that
seem to emanate love and saintliness. . . . [They] will use the word
angel if they are asked for synonyms for these beings of light. I think
the idea is of a helper, a person who is there to assist them through
this experience, and to help them understand so that they won't be
left alone at this moment of transition.

RAYMOND MOODY

*G*o with me like good angels to my end,
And as the long divorce of steel falls on me,
Make of your prayers one sweet sacrifice,
And lift my soul to heaven.

WILLIAM SHAKESPEARE
HENRY VIII

*S*ince there are always yearnings for Apocalypse and fears and
dread of Apocalypse coming together, I think it is inevitable that
angels and everything associated with angels have this enormous
popular revival.

HAROLD BLOOM

*T*he angel of death would be unlikely to arrive with socks to darn.

JENNIFER PRUDENCE JOHNSTON
THE CAPTAINS AND THE KINGS

I looked over Jordan and what did I see?
A band of Angels coming after me;
Comin' for to carry me home.
Swing low sweet chariot.

AFRICAN-AMERICAN SPIRITUAL

*W*hile the angels, all pallid and wan,
Uprising, unveiling, affirm
That the play is the tragedy, "Man,"
and its hero the Conqueror Worm.

EDGAR ALLAN POE

All has been looted, betrayed, sold; black death's wing flashed ahead.

ANNA AKHMATOVA

The stranger rode beside her, easily, lightly, his reins loose in his half-closed hand, straight and elegant in dark shabby garments that flapped upon his bones; his pale face smiled in an evil trance, he did not glance at her. Ah, I have seen this fellow before, I know this man if I could place him. He is no stranger to me.

KATHERINE ANN PORTER
PALE HORSE, PALE RIDER

He mourns that day so soon has glided by:
E'en like the passage of an angel's tear
That falls through the clear ether silently.

JOHN KEATS

Whenever a child dies, an angel comes down from heaven, takes the child in its arms, and spreading out its large white wings, visits all the places that had been particularly dear to the child. From the best-loved place the angel gathers a handful of flowers, flying up again to heaven with them. There they bloom more beautifully than on earth. But that flower which is most loved receives a voice, so that it can join the song of the chorus of bliss.

HANS CHRISTIAN ANDERSEN

What will they do when the angels carry off their souls, striking their faces and their backs?

THE KORAN

They buried him, but all through the night of mourning, in the lighted windows, his books arranged three by three kept watch like angels with outspread wings and seemed, for him who was no more, the symbol of his resurrection.

MARCEL PROUST
THE CAPTIVE

Good Lord in that Heaven,
I know I gotta home at last!
Go, Angel, and tell the news,
Go, Sister, and tell the news,
Go, Elder, and tell the news,
I know I gotta home at last!

EVA A. JESSYE
MY SPIRITUALS

The road is not clear! You're sick as cats! You've made the bomb your god and you're praying for the bomb to call in the number. Well, you'll get it if you don't watch out. The Archangel Gabriel will announce the second coming of the Son of Man, and this time his voice will be a siren. Oh, I get so angry with everyone. Look how foolish I am.

LANFORD WILSON
ANGELS FALL

It may be that Death's bright angel
    Will speak in that chord again,–
It may be that only in Heaven
    I shall hear that grand Amen.

ADELAIDE ANNE PROCTOR
"A LOST CHORD"

To think a soul so near divine,
With a form, so angel fair,
United to a heart like thine,
Has gladdened once our humble sphere.

ANNE BRONTE
"A REMINISCENCE"

I intend to die in a tavern; let the wine be placed near my dying mouth, so that when the choirs of angels come, they may say, "God be merciful to this drinker!"

WALTER MAP

I began to live in your house, and after I had lived with you a year the man came to order the boots which should be strong enough to last him a year without ripping or wearing out of shape. And I looked at him, and suddenly perceived behind his back my comrade, the Angel of Death. No one besides myself saw this angel; but I know him, and I know that before the sun should go down he would take the rich man's soul. And I said to myself, "This man is laying his plans to live another year, and he knows not that ere evening comes he will be dead."

LEO TOLSTOY
"WHAT MEN LIVE BY"

. . . And undoubtedly because of a change of heart by the Angel of Death himself (a figure of fancy to me, but a very serious reality to Old World believers), Bubbeh survived the pneumonia, and she even survived the stroke. Perhaps our tears and our prayers were more important than Harvey's mouth-operated suction device and the residual shreds of strength in that wheezing immune system of hers.

SHERWIN B. NULAND
HOW WE DIE

*E*ach corse lay flat, lifeless and flat,
And, by the holy rood!
A man all light, a seraph-man,
On every corse there stood.

SAMUEL TAYLOR COLERIDGE
"THE RIME OF THE ANCIENT MARINER"

I always thought I'd like my tombstone to be blank. No epitaph, and
no name. Well actually, I'd like it to say "Figment."

ANDY WARHOL

Dark Angels

Angels are bright still, though the brightest fell.

WILLIAM SHAKESPEARE
MACBETH

I gazed intently down, my master said,
"Within the flames are spirits; each one here
Enfolds himself in what burns him."

DANTE ALIGHIERI
INFERNO, CANTO XXVI

The sin, both of men and of angels, was rendered possible by the fact that God gave them free will.

C. S. LEWIS
MIRACLES

An elderly fallen angel traveling incognito.

PETER QUENNELL
SPEAKING OF ANDRE GIDE

*L*ost Angel of a ruined Paradise!
She knew not 'twas her own; as with no stain
She faded, like a cloud which had outwept its rain.

PERCY BYSSHE SHELLEY
ADONAIS

[*J*osef von Sternberg] liked this title [*The Blue Angel*] for it con-
veyed a kind of romantic melancholy in English and another mood
altogether in German, in which *blue* is slang for *drunk*. A heavenly
creature drunk with love, or with self-love, or with love-making,
who could act and sing and speak English and captivate the camera
and bring Emil Jannings low with a song.

STEVEN BACH
MARLENE DIETRICH

*T*he devil is an angel too.

MIGUEL DE UNAMUNO
TWO MOTHERS

*B*ut oh, how fall'n! How changed
From him who, in the happy realms of light,
Clothed with transcendent brightness, didst outshine
Myriads though bright!

JOHN MILTON
PARADISE LOST

"*W*ho art thou, then?"
"Part of that Power, not understood,
Which always wills the Bad, and always works the Good."

JOHANN WOLFGANG VON GOETHE
FAUST

*S*atan, being thus confined to a vagabond, wandering, unsettled condition, is without any certain abode; for though he has, in consequence of his angelic nature, a kind of empire in the liquid waste or air, yet this is certainly part of his punishment, that he is . . . without any fixed place, or space, allowed him to rest the sole of his foot upon.

DANIEL DEFOE
THE HISTORY OF THE DEVIL

*T*he fiend with all his comrades
Fell then from heaven above,
Through as long as three nights and days,
The angels from heaven into hell;
And them all the Lord transformed to devils,
Because they his deed and word
Would not revere.

CAEDMON
"CREATION: THE FALL OF THE REBEL ANGELS"

*M*y cool judgment is, that if all the other doctrines of devils which have been committed to writing since letters were in the world were collected together in one volume, it would fall short of this; and that, should a Prince form himself by this book, so calmly recommending hypocrasy, treachery, lying, robbery, oppression, adultery, whoredom, and murder of all kinds, Domitian or Nero would be an angel of light compared to that man.

JOHN WESLEY
IN A JOURNAL ENTRY MADE AFTER READING
THE WORKS OF NICHOLAS MACHIAVEL, JANUARY 26, 1737

*T*hough an angel should write, still 'tis *devils* must print.

THOMAS MOORE

Let's write "good angel" on the devil's horn,
'Tis not the devil's crest.

WILLIAM SHAKESPEARE
MEASURE FOR MEASURE

From ghoulies and ghosties and
Long-leggety beasties
And things that go bump in the night,
Good lord, deliver us!

SCOTTISH PRAYER

And no marvel; for Satan himself is transformed into an angel of
light. Therefore it is no great thing if his ministers also be transformed as the ministers of righteousness; whose end shall be accord-
ing to their works.

II CORINTHIANS 11:14-15

Dark Angel, with thine aching lust
To rid the world of penitence:
Malicious Angel, who still dost
My soul such subtile violence!

LIONEL JOHNSON
"THE DARK ANGEL"

So when the Angel of the darker Drink
At last shall find you by the river-brink

RUBAIYAT OF OMAR KHAYYAM

Giving the devil his due will always jostle the angels.

R. LANCE HILL
"THE EVIL THAT MEN DO"

Heathen n. A benighted creature who has the folly to worship something that he can see and feel.

AMBROSE BIERCE
THE DEVIL'S DICTIONARY

*W*hat guardian angels are to those who live righteously, imps are to those who follow Satan.

ROBERT MASELLO
FALLEN ANGELS

*D*oes the devil know he is a devil?

ELIZABETH MADOX ROBERTS

*I*t ages the young, and the bloom
Of the maiden is ashes of roses—
    The Swamp Angel broods in his gloom.

HERMAN MELVILLE

*T*o win my soon to hell, my female evil
Tempteth my better angel from my side,
And would corrupt my saint to be a devil,
Wooing his purity with her foul pride.
And whether that my angel be turn'd fiend
Suspect I may, yet not directly tell.

WILLIAM SHAKESPEARE
SONNET 144

*W*hat make ole Satan hate me so? O yes, Lord!
Because he got me once and he let me go, O yes, Lord!

AFRICAN-AMERICAN SPIRITUAL
"NOBODY KNOWS THE TROUBLE I'VE HAD"

*J*udas forced himself to laugh. Then he spat on the ground and shouted, "Eh, son of Carpenter, you're not putting anything over on me—no! Your guardian angel came during the night."

NIKOS KAZANTZAKIS
THE LAST TEMPTATION OF CHRIST

*A*gain, the devil taketh him up into an exceeding high mountain, and sheweth him all the kingdoms of the world, and the glory of them; And saith unto him, All these things will I give thee, if thou wilt fall down and worship me. Then saith Jesus unto him, Get thee hence, Satan: for it is written, Thou shalt worship the Lord thy God, and him only shalt thou serve. Then the devil leaveth him, and, behold, angels came and ministered unto him.

MATTHEW 4:8–10

*I*t is harder for men of this century to believe in the Devil than to love him.

CHARLES BAUDELAIRE

*A*ngels with Dirty Faces

MICHAEL CURTIZ
FILM TITLE

*A*nd they are mingled with angels of that base sort
    Who, neither rebellious to God nor faithful to Him,
Chose neither side, but kept themselves apart—
    Now Heaven expels them, not to mar its splendor,
    And Hell rejects them, lest the wicked of heart
Take glory over them.

DANTE ALIGHIERI
INFERNO, CANTO III

*A*nd there was war in heaven: Michael and his angels fought
against the dragon; and the dragon fought and his angels, And pre-
vailed not; neither was their place found any more in heaven. And
the great dragon was cast out, that old serpent, called the Devil, and
Satan, which deceiveth the whole world: he was cast out into the
earth, and his angels were cast out with him.

REVELATION 12:7–9

      *H*ail horrours, hail
Infernal world, and thou profoundest Hell
Receive thy new Possessor; One who brings
A mind not to be chang'd by Place or Time.
The mind is its own place, and in it self
Can make a Heav'n of Hell, a Hell of Heav'n.
What matter where, if I be still the same,
And what should I be, all but less than he
Whom thunder hath made greater? Here at least
We shall be free; th' Almighty hath not built
Here for his envy, will not drive us hence:
Here we may reign secure, and in my choice
To reign is worth ambition though in Hell:
Better to reign in Hell, than serve in Heav'n.

JOHN MILTON
PARADISE LOST

*T*ruth will I speak, repeat it to the living;
   God's Angel took me up, and he of hell
   Shouted: 'O thou from heaven, why dost thou
      rob me?

DANTE ALIGHIERI
PURGATORIO, CANTO V

III

Angels Infuse Our Perception

Of Human Nature and Angels

*W*hat a piece of work is man, how noble in reason, how
infinite in faculties, in form and moving, how express and
admirable in action, how like an angel in apprehension, how
like a god! the beauty of the world; the paragon of animals;
and yet to me what is this quintessence of dust? Man
delights not me.

WILLIAM SHAKESPEARE
HAMLET

*P*eople are not fallen angels, they are merely people.

D. H. LAWRENCE
IN A LETTER TO J. MIDDLETON MURRY AND KATHERINE MANSFIELD

*S*ometimes it is said that man cannot be trusted with the government of himself. Can he, then, be trusted with the government of
others? Or have we found angels in the forms of kings to govern
him? Let history answer this question.

THOMAS JEFFERSON
IN HIS 1ST INAUGURAL ADDRESS, MARCH 4, 1801

*H*e who is unable to live in society, or who has no need because he is sufficient for himself, must be either a beast or a god.

ARISTOTLE
POLITICS

*B*ut we were born of risen apes, not fallen angels . . .

ROBERT ARDREY
AFRICAN GENESIS

I! I who fashioned myself a sorcerer or an angel, who dispensed with all morality, I have come back to the earth.

ARTHUR RIMBAUD

*M*an is no angel. He is sometimes more of a hypocrite and some-times less, and then fools say that he has or has not principles.

HONORE DE BALZAC

*T*oo much liberty corrupts an angel.

TERENCE (PUBLIUS TERENTIUS AFER)

*W*hat is government itself but the greatest of all reflections on human nature? If men were angels, no government would be neces-sary. If angels were to govern men, neither external nor internal controls on government would be necessary.

JAMES MADISON
THE FEDERALIST

*W*e are not enemies, but friends. We must not be enemies. Though passion may have strained, it must not break, our bonds of affection. The mystic chords of memory, stretching from every battlefield, and patriot grave, to every living heart and hearthstone, all over this broad land, will yet swell the chorus of the Union, when again touched, as surely they will be, by the better angels of our nature.

ABRAHAM LINCOLN
IN HIS 1ST INAUGURAL ADDRESS, MARCH 4, 1861

*O*ur deeds fashion our destiny.
Heaven and Hell are in our own hands.

HILLEL

*T*here are only two ways to live your life. One is as though nothing is a miracle. The other is as though everything is a miracle.

ALBERT EINSTEIN

I watched pigeons flying past the little well at the cloister in San Francisco, and forgot my thirst. But a moment always came when I was thirsty again.

ALBERT CAMUS
"LOVE OF LIFE"

*T*here is little leisure to discover what lies around us, and so much—presumably—for what is beyond; and it has long seemed to me to be the behaviour of a rather ill-mannered guest on this planet, to wolf his earlier courses and ask for port and coffee straightaway.

FREYA STARK
BEYOND EUPHRATES

LOVE CALLS US TO THE THINGS OF THIS WORLD

The eyes open to a cry of pulleys,
And spirited from sleep, the astounded soul
Hangs for a moment bodiless and simple
As false dawn.
              Outside the open window
The morning air is all awash with angels.

       Some are in bed-sheets, some are in blouses,
Some are in smocks: but truly there they are.
Now they are rising together in calm swells
Of halcyon feeling, filling whatever they wear
With the deep joy of their impersonal breathing;

       Now they are flying in place, conveying
The terrible speed of their omnipresence, moving
And staying like white water; and now of a sudden
They swoon down into so rapt a quiet
That nobody seems to be there.
              The soul shrinks

       From all that it is about to remember,
From the punctual rape of every blessed day,
and cries,
       "Oh, let there be nothing on earth but laundry,
Nothing but rosy hands in the rising steam
And clear dances done in the sight of heaven."

       Yet, as the sun acknowledges
With a warm look the world's hunks and colors,
The soul descends once more in bitter love
To accept the waking body, saying now
In a changed voice as the man yawns and rises,

       "Bring them down from their ruddy gallows;
Let there be clean linen for the backs of thieves;
Let lovers go fresh and sweet to be undone,
And the heaviest nuns walk in a pure floating
Of dark habits,
              keeping their difficult balance.'

RICHARD WILBUR

I neglect God and his angels for the noise of a fly, for the rattling of a coach, for the whining of a door.

JOHN DONNE

[*A*ngels are] a New Age answer to the homelessness of secularity.

TED PETERS

*T*he interest in angels is about not wanting to die.

HAROLD BLOOM

I want to be an angel,
   And with the angels stand
A crown upon my forehead,
   A harp within my hand.

URANIA LOCKE BAILEY

*I*n a picture I want to say something comforting as music is comforting. I want to paint men and women with that something of the eternal which the halo used to symbolize, and which we seek to give by the actual radiance and vibration of our colorings . . .

VINCENT VAN GOGH

*T*hat melancholy and industrious animal—man—may discover new forces and harness them to his chariot. Some such danger is in the air. The result will be a great abundance—of human beings!
Every square yard will be occupied by a man. Who will be able then to cure us of the lack of air and space? The mere thought of it suffocates me.

ITALO SVEVO
CONFESSIONS OF ZENO

I have never admired being human, I must say. I want to be like God. But I haven't begun yet. First I have to go to Massachusetts and be alone.

JANE BOWLES

*G*ive heed then, you hearers,
and you also, angels and those who have been sent,
and you spirits risen now from the dead.
I am the one who alone exists,
there is no one to judge me.

GNOSTIC GOSPEL

*A*ngels fall, they are towers, from heaven—a story
Of just, majestical, and giant groans.
But man—we, scaffold of score brittle bones;
Who breathe, from groundlong babyhood to hoary
Age grasp; whose breath is our *memento mori*—
What bass is *our* viol for tragic tones?

GERARD MANLEY HOPKINS

*I*s man an ape or an angel? My lord, I am on the side of the angels.

BEJAMIN DISRAELI

A fine thing to be talking about angels in this day when common thieves smash the holy rosaries of their victims in the street . . .

JACK KEROUAC
DESOLATION ANGELS

By philosophy man realizes the virtual characteristics of his race. He attains the form of humanity and progresses on the hierarchy of beings until in crossing the straight way (or "bridge") and the correct path, he becomes an Angel.

BRETHREN OF PURITY
RISALAT AL-JAMI'AH

I have always found that Angels have the vanity to speak of themselves as the only wise; this they do with a confident insolence sprouting from systematic reasoning.

WILLIAM BLAKE
"THE MARRIAGE OF HEAVEN AND HELL"

If the notion of a gradual rise in beings from the meanest to the most high be not a vain imagination, it is not improbable that an angel looks down upon a man, as a man doth upon a creature which approaches the nearest to the rational nature.

JOSEPH ADDISON

Man is neither angel nor brute, and the unfortunate thing is that he who would act the angel acts the brute.

BLAISE PASCAL

We were made to be neither cerebral men nor visceral men, but Men. Not beasts nor angels but Men—things at once rational and animal.

C. S. LEWIS
THE PILGRIM'S REGRESS

There's a young man hid with me, in comparison with which young man I am a Angel. That young man hears the words I speak. That young man has a secret way pecooliar to himself, of getting at a boy, and at his heart, and at his liver.

CHARLES DICKENS
GREAT EXPECTATIONS

Where is one to find the images that humankind has created to give itself a direction, a goal toward which to aspire? . . . There are so many depictions of gods, angels, demons, and anthropomorphic animals that are tempting to use as models, but that ultimately must be rejected as irrelevant.

MIHALY CSIKSZENTMIHALYI
THE EVOLVING SELF

There's a divinity that shapes our ends,
Rough-hew them how we will.

WILLIAM SHAKESPEARE
HAMLET

He is not Old Brown any longer; he is an angel of light.

HENRY DAVID THOREAU
A PLEA FOR CAPTAIN JOHN BROWN

When I consider thy heavens, the work of thy fingers, the moon and the stars, which thou hast ordained; What is man, that thou art mindful of him? and the son of man, that thou visitest him? For thou has made him a little lower than the angels, and has crowned him with glory and honour.

PSALMS 8:3–5

Neither the Bible nor the prophets—neither Freud nor research—neither the revelations of God nor man—can take precedence over my own direct experience.

CARL ROGERS

Those sweetly smiling angels with pensive looks, innocent faces, and cash-boxes for hearts.

HONORE DE BALZAC
COUSIN BETTE

When they count my sins in heaven, then I'll get to know my luck
Is it furnace number seven or a harp for me to pluck?

BERTOLT BRECHT
HAPPY END

How should we like it were stars to burn
With a passion for us we could not return?
If equal affection cannot be,
Let the more loving one be me.

W. H. AUDEN
"THE MORE LOVING ONE"

*I*n the
*G*arden

I believe a leaf of grass is no less than the journey-work of the stars . . .

WALT WHITMAN

*T*he heaventree of stars hung with humid nightblue fruit.

JAMES JOYCE
ULYSSES

*A*ngel-duck, angel-duck, winged and silly,
Pouring a watering-pot over a lily.

CHARLES LAMB

*W*hat angel wakes me from my flowery bed?

WILLIAM SHAKESPEARE
A MIDSUMMER NIGHT'S DREAM

*T*he awakening of consciousness is not unlike the crossing of a
frontier—one step and you are in another country.

ADRIENNE RICH

*I*n either hand the hastening angel caught
Our lingering parents, and to the eastern gate
Led them direct, and down the cliff as fast
To the subjected plain; then disappeared.
They, looking back, all the eastern side beheld
Of Paradise, so late their happy seat,
Waved over by that flaming brand; the gate
With dreadful faces thronged and fiery arms.
Some natural tears they dropt, but wiped them soon;
The world was all before them, where to choose
Their place of rest, and Providence their guide.
They, hand in hand, with wandering steps and slow,
Through Eden took their solitary way.

JOHN MILTON
PARADISE LOST

Angel's trumpet n. A common name for several different plants:
Brugmansia suaveolens, *B. arborea*, and red angel's trumpet, *B. sanguinea*, as well as *Datura inoxia*. *Brugmansia* spp. are tropical or
subtropical shrubs or small trees with trumpet-shaped flowers 6 to
20 inches long, all richly fragrant at night except *B. sanguinea*. *D.
inoxia* is a spiny perennial herb, 3-feet high, with 8-inch-long pink
or lavender trumpet-shaped flowers.

THE NATIONAL GARDENING ASSOCIATION
DICTIONARY OF HORTICULTURE

*A*nd on Angel Landing, the point jutting out from the far side of
the harbor, where there had once been thousands of shells called
false angel wings, a nuclear power plant was being built. The metal
scales of Angel Landing III now rose into the sky with the terrible
force of centuries.

ALICE HOFFMAN
ANGEL LANDING

To whom the winged Hierarch replied:
O Adam, one Almighty is, from whom
All things proceed.

DANTE ALIGHIERI
PARADISO, CANTO V

There appeared to me very beautiful rainbows, as on former occasions, but still more beautiful, with a light of the purest white, in the
centre of which was an obscure earthly something; but that most
lucid snow-white appearance was beautifully varied by another
lucidity . . . and, if I rightly recollect, with flowers of different colors
round about.

EMANUEL SWENDENBORG

*W*ho can order the Holy? It is like a rain forest, dripping, lush, fecund, wild. We enter its abundance at our peril, for here we are called to the wholeness for which we belong, but which requires all we are and can hope to be.

MARILYN SEWELL
CRIES OF THE SPIRIT

*A*nd, as I took part in this dance and joined in the chant myself, it was not hard for me to imagine that such an unearthly ritual must be placating some unearthly force.

RICHARD EVANS SCHULTES

I am sure there is Magic in everything, only we have not sense enough to get hold of it and make it do things for us.

FRANCES HODGES BURNETT
THE SECRET GARDEN

*R*oses of sunshine, vilets of dew,
Angels in heaven knows I love you.

AFRICAN-AMERICAN SPIRITUAL
"DOWN IN THE VALLEY"

*M*y delight and thy delight
Walking, like two angels white,
In the gardens of the night

ROBERT BRIDGES

Till another open for me
In God's Eden-land unknown
With an angel at the doorway

ELIZABETH BARRETT BROWNING
"THE LOST BOWER"

Surely the strange beauty of the world must somewhere rest on
pure joy!

LOUISE BOGAN

My father explained this to me. "All things in this world," he said,
"have souls or spirits. The sky has a spirit, the clouds have spirits;
the sun and moon have spirits; so have animals, trees, grass, water,
stars, *everything.*"

EDWARD GOODBIRD

Nor in that place had nature painted only,
    But of the sweetness of a thousand odors
    Made there a mingled fragrance and unknown.
    "Salve Regina," on the green and flowers
    There seated, singing, spirits I beheld,
    Which were not visible outside the valley.

DANTE ALIGHIERI
PURGATORIO, CANTO VII

_A_ngel Voices

_W_rit in the climate of heaven, in the language spoken by angels.

HENRY WADSWORTH LONGFELLOW
"THE CHILDREN OF THE LORD'S SUPPER"

_A_nd the angel Israfel, whose heart-strings are a lute, and who has the sweetest voice of all God's creatures.

THE KORAN

_T_he bell strikes one: we take no note of time,
But from its loss. To give it, then, a tongue,
Is wise in man. As if an angel spoke,
I feel the solemn sound.

DR. EDWARD YOUNG
"TIME"

_I_ grew up as a female who heard voices.

LUCILLE CLIFTON

The angel ended, and in Adam's ear
So charming left his voice that he awhile
Thought him still speaking, still stood fix'd to hear.

JOHN MILTON
PARADISE LOST

All night I could not sleep
because of the moonlight on my bed.
I kept on hearing a voice calling:
Out of Nowhere, Nothing answered "yes."

TSU YEH

Par le parler et le langaige des angles

JEANNE D'ARC

Spirit-noiseless

FORCEYTHE WILLSON

All round the circle of the sky I hear the Spirit's voice.

NATIVE AMERICAN SAYING

Learn to listen. Opportunity sometimes knocks very softly.

H. JACKSON BROWN, JR.
LIFE'S LITTLE INSTRUCTION BOOK

If we have listening ears, God speaks to us in our own language,
whatever that language is.

GANDHI
MOHANDAS KARAMCHAND (MAHATMA)

To catch even the echo of a thousand times
weakened and repeated of the authentic voice
of happiness, is worth a journey.

FREYA STARK

And I beheld, and I heard the voice of many
angels round about the throne and the beasts
and the elders: and the number of them was
ten thousand times ten thousand, and thousands of thousands.

REVELATION 5:11

I have seen a thousand times that angels are
human forms, or men, for I have conversed
with them as man to man, sometimes with one
alone, sometimes with many in company.

EMANUEL SWENDENBORG

The extraterrestrials can't say things directly.
They have to express themselves in an indirect
way, a figurative way—for example, through
stories that arouse unusual emotions.

ITALO CALVINO
IF ON A WINTER'S NIGHT A TRAVELER

The Gaze of
an Angel

The brute curiosity of an angel's stare
Turns you like them into stone.

ALLEN TATE

Look homeward, Angel, now, and melt with ruth.

JOHN MILTON
"Lycidas"

And the angels on Grant's porch were frozen in hard marble silence, and at a distance life awoke, and there was a rattle of lean wheels, a slow clangor of shod hoofs. And he heard the whistle wail along the river.

Yet, as he stood for the last time by the angels of his father's porch, it seemed as if the Square already were far and lost; or, I should say, he was like a man who stands upon a hill above the town he has left, yet does not say "The town is near," but turns his eyes upon the distant soaring ranges.

THOMAS WOLFE
Look Homeward, Angel

Minute after minute, aeon after aeon,
Nothing lets up or develops.
And this is neither a bad variant nor a tryout.
This is where the staring angels go through.
This is where all the stars bow down.

TED HUGHES
"PIBROCH"

Yet I am the necessary angel of earth,
Since, in my sight, you see the earth again

WALLACE STEVENS
"ANGEL SURROUNDED BY PAYSANS"

An angel of Paradise, no less, is always beside me, wrapped in
everlasting ecstasy on his Lord. So I am ever under the gaze of an
angel who protects and prays for me.

POPE JOHN XXIII

Satotteiru <u>kao</u>
a <u>face</u> that is enlightened

JOHN LENNON

Here eyes like angels watch them still;
    Her brows like bended bows do stand,
Threatening with piercing frowns to kill
    All that attempt with eye or hand
Those sacred cherries to come nigh,
    Till 'Cherry-ripe' themselves do cry.

THOMAS CAMPION
"CHERRY-RIPE"

*B*ut, Lord, as burnish't Sun Beams forth out fly
   Let Angell-shine forth in my life out flame

EDWARD TAYLOR

"*W*hat aileth thee, that aye to earth thou gazest?"
To me my Guide began to say, we both
Somewhat beyond the Angel having mounted.

DANTE ALIGHIERI
PURGATORIO, CANTO XIX

Angels of the Natural World

*S*he knew things that nobody had ever told her. For instance, the words of the trees and the wind. She often spoke to falling seeds and said, "Ah hope you fall on the ground," because she had heard seeds saying that to each other as they passed.

ZORA NEALE HURSTON
THEIR EYES WERE WATCHING GOD

*I*nspiration is 95% nature and silence.

ALICE WALKER

*A*n angel, robed in spotless white,
Bent down and kissed the sleeping Night,
Night woke to blush; the sprite was gone,
Men saw the blush and called it Dawn.

PAUL LAURENCE DUNBAR

*E*very raindrop that falls is accompanied by an Angel, for even a raindrop is a manifestation of being.

MOHAMMED

$\mathcal{A}$ngels, in the early morning
May be seen the Dews among
Stooping–plucking–smiling–flying–
Do the Buds to them belong?

Angels, when the sun is hottest
May be seen the sands among,
Stooping–plucking–sighing–flying–
Parched the flowers they bear along.

EMILY DICKINSON

$\mathcal{H}$ey, angel," Amarante called out in his dream. "What's a rainbow
doing over our town on a sunny day like today?"

JOHN NICHOLS
THE MILAGRO BEANFIELD WAR

Angel's-tears n. A common name applied to plants of 3 genera: *Datura sanguinea*, a tropical shrub or small tree; *Narcissus triandrus*, a miniature daffodil; and *Soleirolia Soleirolii*, a shade-loving ground cover.

THE NATIONAL GARDENING ASSOCIATION
DICTIONARY OF HORTICULTURE

*N*ature, which has established a chain of being and a universal order in the universe, descending from the angels to microscopic animalcules, has ordained that no two objects shall be perfectly alike and no two creatures perfectly equal.

JOHN ADAMS

*H*ad I offered sacrifices to little forest divinities, it would have been fully in keeping with my nature. I would have been aware that my behavior was absurd but, even more, that it was right because a sense of oneness with those forces we know exist but are unable to name demands symbolic gestures. Perhaps I am exaggerating, but all those dawns and twilights spent watching for birds, and all my child-hood memories of the dangers of war, did not dispose me to a belief in chance.

CZESLAW MILOSZ
NATIVE REALM

I was listening to the voices of life chanting in unison.

JOHN TRUDELL

*E*arth being so good, would Heaven be best?

ROBERT BROWNING

*I*f you want to tell anything to God, tell it to the wind.

AFRICAN PROVERB

*W*e're dealing with primal forces of nature here. When primal forces of nature tell you to do something the prudent thing is not to quibble over details.

KEVIN COSTNER
AS RAY KINSELLA IN PHIL ALDEN ROBINSON'S FIELD OF DREAMS

*A*nimists believe that there are all kinds of active little gods lurking in rocks and caves, birds and beasts, in the waters and in the forests. In other words, they believe that the whole world is animate—alive—with divinity. Although it can give rise to enslaving superstition, animism may not be that far from the mark.

M. SCOTT PECK
IN SEARCH OF STONES

In our description of nature the purpose is not to disclose the real essence of the phenomena but only to track down, so far as it is possible, relations between the manifold aspects of our experience.

NIELS BOHR

Yea, ape and angel, strife and old debate—
The harps of heaven and dreary gongs of hell;
Science the feud can only aggravate—
No umpire she betwixt the chimes and knell:
The running battle of the star and clod
Shall run forever—if there be no God.

HERMAN MELVILLE

Christianity desacralized nature and drew an impassable line dividing the natural and the human. The nymphs fled, the naiads, satyrs, and Tritons were turned into angels or demons. The modern age accentuated the divorce: at one extreme, nature, and at the other, culture. Today, as modernity comes to an end, we are rediscovering that we are part of nature.

OCTAVIO PAZ
THE DOUBLE FLAME

Nothing from nothing ever yet was born.
Fear holds dominion over mortality
Only because, seeing in land and sky
So much the cause whereof no wise they know,
Men think Divinities are working there.

LUCRETIUS

The spirits of the sun-place have whispered them words.

HAWK CHANT OF THE SAGINAWS

*G*od said, Let there be light; and there was light.
Then heard we sounds as though the Earth did sing
And the Earth's angel cried upon the wing

DANTE GABRIEL ROSSETTI
"AT THE SUN-RISE IN 1848"

*T*he heavens were inhabited by angels, demons, and the Hand of God, turning the planetary crystal spheres. Science was barren of the idea that underlying the phenomena of Nature might be the laws of physics.

CARL SAGAN
COSMOS

*W*e were contented to let things remain as the Great Spirit made them.

CHIEF JOSEPH

I have been to the end of the earth.
I have been to the end of the waters.
I have been to the end of the sky.
I have been to the end of the mountains.
I have found none that were not my friends.

NAVAJO CHANT

*T*here's no rush about calling things sacred. I think we should be patient, and give the land a lot of time to tell us or the people of the future. The cry of a Flicker, the funny urgent chatter of a Gray Squirrel, the acorn whack on a barn roof—are signs enough.

GARY SNYDER
"GOOD, WILD, SACRED"

And after these things I saw four angels standing on the four corners of the earth, holding the four winds of the earth, that the wind should not blow on the earth, nor on the sea, nor on any tree.

REVELATION 7:1

The hills are steeped in Cosmic regrets and the valleys are flooded with morose and aimless puddles.

ZELDA FITZGERALD
IN A LETTER TO SCOTT, 1939

His imagined birds, and painted bowl,
　And venison, for a journey dressed,
Bespeak the nature of his soul,
　Activity, that knows no rest.

PHILIP FRENEAU
"THE INDIAN BURYING GROUND"

*P*rayer and *A*ngels

*P*rayer, the Church's banquet, Angels' age,
　　God's breath in man returning to his birth,
The soul in paraphrase, heart in pilgrimage.

GEORGE HERBERT
"PRAYER"

O waste of loss, in the hot mazes, lost, among bright stars on this most weary unbright cinder, lost! Remembering speechlessly we seek the great forgotten language, the lost lane-end into heaven, a stone, a leaf, an unfound door. Where? When?
　　O lost, and by the wind grieved, ghost, come back again.

THOMAS WOLFE
LOOK HOMEWARD, ANGEL

*H*oly Angels, our advocates, our brothers, our counselors, our defenders, our enlighteners, our friends, our guides, our helpers, our intercessors—Pray for us.

MOTHER TERESA

*W*hen anyone prays, the angels that minister to God and watch over mankind gather round about him and join with him in prayer.

ORIGEN

*F*ather expected a good deal of God. He didn't actually accuse God of inefficiency, but when he prayed his tone was loud and angry, like that of a dissatisfied guest in a carelessly managed hotel.

CLARENCE DAY

*T*hen Jesus said unto him, Put up thy sword into his place: for all they that take the sword shall perish with the sword. Thinkest thou that I cannot now pray to my Father, and he shall presently give me more than twelve legions of angels? But how then shall the scriptures be fulfilled, that thus it must be?

MATTHEW 26:53–54

*I*f prayers worked, Hitler would have been stopped at the border of Poland by angels with swords of fire.

NANCY WILLARD
THINGS INVISIBLE TO SEE

*C*hristian, seek not yet repose,
Hear thy guardian angel say,
"Thou art in the midst of foes;
Watch and pray."

CHARLOTTE ELLIOTT

*B*ut if these beings guard you, they do so because they have been summoned by your prayers.

ST. AMBROSE

*S*weet souls around us watch us still,
   Press nearer to our side;
Into our thoughts, into our prayers,
   With gentle helpings guide.

HARRIET BEECHER STOWE
"THE OTHER WORLD"

*M*atthew, Mark, Luke, and John,
The bed be blest that I lie on.
Four angels to my bed,
Four angels round my head,
One to watch, and one to pray,
And two to bear my soul away.

THOMAS ADY
"A CANDLE IN THE DARK"

*T*he part about maybe dying before waking had worried him. So did the angelic pallbearers standing ready to haul him away. It was hard to get to sleep under these conditions. . . . He imagined he was going off to see God. And the last thing he remembered thinking was, "If I die before I wake, how would I ever know or care? Amen."
   And he slept through till morning.
   When he checked the mirror in the bathroom, he was still there.

ROBERT FULGHUM
FROM BEGINNING TO END

And he was withdrawn from them about a stone's cast, and kneeled down, and prayed, Saying, Father, if thou be willing, remove this cup from me: nevertheless not my will, but thine, be done. And there appeared an angel unto him from heaven, strengthening him.

LUKE 22:41-43

When ol' Sis' Judy pray,
Salvation's light come pourin' down—
Hit fill de chu'ch an' all de town—
Why, angels' robes go rustlin' 'roun',
An' hebben on de Yurf am foun',
When ol' Sis' Judy pray.

JAMES EDWIN CAMPBELL

The breeze at dawn has secrets to tell you.
           Don't go back to sleep.
You must ask for what you really want.
           Don't go back to sleep.
People are going back and forth across the doorsill
           where the two worlds touch.
The door is round and open.
           Don't go back to sleep.

JALALUDDIN RUMI

The man who sat on the ground in his tipi meditating on life and its meaning, accepting the kinship of all creatures and acknowledging unity with the universe of things, was infusing into his being the true essence of civilization.

CHIEF LUTHER STANDING BEAR

Bless the Lord, ye his angels, that excel in strength, that do his commandments, hearkening unto the voice of his word.

PSALMS 103:20

Wrestling with Angels

*W*e cannot part with our friends; we cannot let our angels go.

RALPH WALDO EMERSON
"COMPENSATION"

*H*old the fleet angel fast until he bless thee.

NATHANIEL COTTON

I locked myself in my room. The moon shone on the angel's terrace. The curtain would soon rise on the last act of the day. As I looked out on the terrace I remembered that the angel was missing its nose. The anarchists had broken it off with a stone on that First of May.

BEATRIZ GUIDO
"THE HOUSE OF THE ANGEL"

*E*ven the clerics were sufficiently hazy on angelology to be at all certain that even an angel might not resent being shot down.

HOWARD FAST
"THE GENERAL ZAPPED AN ANGEL"

Υea Jacob himself when he wrestled with God face to face in Penuel, "Let me go," saith that Angel. "I will not let thee go," replies Jacob, "till thee bless me." Faith is not only thus potent but it is so necessary that without faith there is no salvation; therefore with all our seekings and gettings, let us above all seek to obtain this pearl of price.

ANNE BRADSTREET

$\mathcal{T}$hose whom we cannot catch we leave in the hands of God.

AFRICAN PROVERB

You couldn't hurt an angel but I would have been happy to know I had dirtied his feathers—I conceived of him in feathers.

FLANNERY O'CONNOR
THE HABIT OF BEING

Thus, whenever I felt the shadow of her wing or the radiance of her halo upon my page, I took up the inkpot and flung it at her. She died hard. Her fictitious nature was of great assistance to her. It is far harder to kill a phantom than a reality. She was always creeping back when I thought I had dispatched her. Though I flatter myself that I killed her in the end, the struggle was severe; it took much time that had better have been spent upon learning Greek grammar; or in roaming the world in search of adventures. But it was a real experience; it was an experience that was bound to befall all women writers at that time. Killing the Angel of the House was part of the occupation of a woman writer.

VIRGINIA WOOLF
"PROFESSIONS FOR WOMEN"

A peaceful sorrow at home is the best I'll ever be able to offer the world, in the end, and so I told my Desolation Angels goodbye. A new life for me.

JACK KEROUAC

What is the answer? . . . In that case, what is the question?

GERTRUDE STEIN
LAST WORDS

IV

---

*In Praise of
the Sacred*

The Universe

*I*ndeed, whatever exists in the universe, whether in essence, in act, or in the imagination, the painter has first in his mind and then in his hands.

LEONARDO DA VINCI
THE NOTEBOOKS

I am convinced that the universe is under the control of a loving purpose, and that in the struggle for righteousness man has cosmic companionship. Behind the harsh appearance of the world there is a benign power.

MARTIN LUTHER KING, JR.

*I*t is only for God (the bestower and creator of forms), and perhaps for angels or intelligences at once to recognize forms affirmatively at the first glance of contemplation.

FRANCIS BACON

I accept the universe!

MARGARET FULLER

Being is born of not being.

LAO TZU
TAO TE CHING

The natural history of the mind is no further advanced today than was natural science in the thirteenth century. We have only begun to take scientific note of our spiritual experiences.

C. G. JUNG

The general plan of creation would display a manifest gap, if there were no angels.

ETIENNE GILSON

This feeling of being loved and supported by the Universe in general and by certain recognizable spirits in particular is bliss.

ALICE WALKER

The angels all were singing out of tune,
 And hoarse with having little else to do,
Excepting to wind up the sun and moon,
 Or curb a runaway young star or two.

LORD BYRON
THE VISION OF JUDGEMENT

Sure there is music even in the beauty, and the silent note which Cupid strikes, far sweeter than the sound of an instrument. For there is a music wherever there is a harmony, order, or proportion; and thus far we may maintain the music of the spheres.

SIR THOMAS BROWNE

We cannot doubt that numberless worlds and systems of worlds compose this amazing whole, the universe; and as little, I think, that the planets which roll about the sun, or those which roll about a multitude of others, are inhabited by living creatures, fit to be inhabitants of them. When we have this view before our eyes, can we be stupid or vain or impertinent enough to imagine that we stand alone or foremost among rational created beings?

LORD BOLINGBROKE

Four of these same Seven Arrows are symbolized by the Four Directions. They are North, South, West, and the East . . . They symbolize Wisdom, Trust and Innocence, Introspection, and Illumination. These are known as the four Ways. The Mother Earth is the Fifth Mirror. The Sky, with its Moon, Sun, and Stars, is the Sixth Mirror. The Seventh of these Arrows is the Spirit. Among the People, the Spirit is spoken of as the Universal Harmony which holds all things together. All of us, as Perceivers of the Mirrors, are the Eighth Arrow.

HYEMEYOHSTS STORM

And at the level of meaning, just as rhymes interlock throughout a canto, so do incidents and images throughout the poem. For instance, the already mentioned black hole at the heart of the Earth "rhymes" with the dazzling, atomic, all-engendering point far out in the Primum Mobile, round which the angelic orders revolve and upon which, says Beatrice, "the heavens and all nature are dependent."

JAMES MERRILL
INTRODUCTION TO DANTE'S INFERNO

A cluster of white stars, silvered against the background of the blue velvet sky, force their way into my eyes and into my heart.

MARC CHAGALL

Life, Time, Space, Thought, the World, the Universe
End where they first begin, in one sole thought
Of Purity in Silence.

HENRY ADAMS
"BUDDHA AND BRAHMA"

[Human beings cannot] conceive that somewhere behind the
farthest stars there exists the end of space and a boundary behind
which there is "nothing."

M. C. ESCHER
EXPLORING THE INFINITE

A single lifetime, even though entirely devoted to the sky, would
not be enough for the investigation of so vast a subject.

SENECA
NATURAL QUESTIONS

If it ever entered the mind of a frivolous angel to dance on the head
of a pin, its whimsical impulse would have to be exercised in a solitary fashion. It could not invite other angels to join it. It would have
to dance there alone.

MORTIMER J. ADLER

As long as you are asking for help, you might as well ask for help
from the universe. You never know what might happen.

ELAINE ST. JAMES
INNER SIMPLICITY

To tell us that every species of thing is endowed with an occult specific quality by which it acts and produces manifest effects, is to tell us nothing; but to derive two or three general principles of motion from phenomena, and afterward to tell us how the properties and actions of all corporeal things follow from those manifest principles, would be a very great step.

ISAAC NEWTON
Optics

Do there exist many worlds, or is there but a single world? This is one of the most noble and exalted questions in the study of Nature.

ALBERTUS MAGNUS

The Prince of Peace was anxious to come to earth and an angel was used to bring the good news that the Creator [of the universe] would become a little child.

MOTHER TERESA

And then he shall send his angels, and shall gather together his elect from the four winds, from the uttermost part of the earth to the uttermost part of heaven.

MARK 13:27

The cosmos of the Native North American was, and to a large degree still is, a universe shaped by and viewed through the spirit.

JOSEPH BRUCHAC

$\mathcal{D}$o not think you can love God
and despise creation.
The two are at root One.

RABBI CHANINA

$\mathcal{T}$he question on most people's minds, whether conscious or unconscious is this: What will happen now? From channeled entities
claiming to hail from the Pleiades to fundamentalist Christians, from
the prophecies of Nostradamus to visions of the Virgin Mary, from
angels who whisper to a backwoods carpenter to scientific think
tanks, come predictions of global shift, perhaps cataclysm, in the
years ahead.

MARIANNE WILLIAMSON
ILLUMINATA

$\mathcal{T}$he universe is the harmonious interaction of all the elements that
create balance and harmony. The word *universe* literally means "one
song" (*uni:* one; *verse:* song). In this song, in this harmony, there is
peace, laughter, joy, and bliss.

DEEPAK CHOPRA
CREATING AFFLUENCE: WEALTH CONSCIOUSNESS
IN THE FIELD OF ALL POSSIBILITIES

$\mathcal{F}$or the world and time are the dance of the Lord in emptiness.
The silence of the spheres is the music of a wedding feast. The more
we persist in misunderstanding the phenomena of life, the more we
analyze them out into strange finalities and complex purposes of our
own, the more we involve ourselves in sadness, absurdity, and
despair. But it does not matter much, because no despair of ours can

alter the reality of things, or stain the joy of the cosmic dance which
is always there. Indeed, we are in the midst of it, and it is in the midst
of us, for it beats in our very blood, whether we want it to or not.

THOMAS MERTON
"THE GENERAL DANCE"

The most beautiful and most profound emotion we can experience
is the sensation of the mystical. It is the dower of all true science. He
to whom this emotion is a stranger, who can no longer wonder and
stand rapt in awe, is as good as dead. To know what is impenetrable
to us really exists, manifesting itself as the highest wisdom and the
most radiant beauty which our dull faculties can comprehend only
in their most primitive forms—this knowledge, this feeling is at the
center of true religiousness.

ALBERT EINSTEIN

Where Angels Dwell

*I*t is not known precisely where angels dwell—whether in the air, the void, or the planets. It has not been God's pleasure that we should be informed of their abode.

VOLTAIRE
PHILOSOPHICAL DICTIONARY

*S*ince angels are men, and live together in society like men on earth, therefore they have garments, houses, and other things familiar to those which exist on earth, but, of course, infinitely more beautiful and perfect.

EMANUEL SWEDENBORG

*T*he world has angels all too few,
     And heaven is overflowing . . .

SAMUEL TAYLOR COLERIDGE

*H*eaven is neither a place nor a time.

FLORENCE NIGHTINGALE
MYSTICISM

I have traveled more than anyone else, and I have noticed that even the angels speak English with an accent.

MARK TWAIN
FOLLOWING THE EQUATOR

*W*ho has not found the Heaven—below—
Will fail of it above—
For Angels rent the House next ours,
Wherever we remove—

EMILY DICKINSON

*A*ngels are everywhere distributed about, as officers of the world, with equal power, zeal and kindness.

JOHN COLET

*I*n this unbelievable universe in which we live there are no absolutes. Even parallel lines, reaching into infinity, meet somewhere yonder.

PEARL BUCK
A BRIDGE FOR PASSING

O tribe of spirits and of men, if you are able to slip through the parameters of the skies and the earth, then do so.

THE KORAN

*B*EN, *with promise:* It's dark here, but full of diamonds.

ARTHUR MILLER
DEATH OF A SALESMAN

IN THE LIBRARY

There's a book called
"A Dictionary of Angels."
No one has opened it in fifty years,
I know, because when I did,
The covers creaked, the pages
Crumbled. There I discovered

The angels were once as plentiful
As species of flies.
The sky at dusk
Used to be thick with them.
You had to wave both arms
Just to keep them away.

Now the sun is shining
Through the tall windows.
The library is a quiet place.
Angels and gods huddled
In dark unopened books.
The great secret lies
On some shelf Miss Jones
Passes every day on her rounds.

She's very tall, so she keeps
Her head tipped as if listening.
The books are whispering.
I hear nothing, but she does.

CHARLES SIMIC

People take the figurative language of the Bible and the allegories
for literal, and the first thing they ask for when they get here is a
halo and a harp, and so on. Nothing that's harmless and reasonable
is refused to a body here, if he asks it in the right spirits. So they are
outfitted with these things without a word. They go and sing and
play just about one day, and that's the last you'll ever see them in
the choir. They don't need anybody to tell them that that sort of

thing wouldn't make a heaven—at least not a heaven that a sane man could stand a week and remain sane.

MARK TWAIN
"CAPTAIN STORMFIELD'S VISIT TO HEAVEN"

Let seraph's gain the bright abode,
And heaven's sublimest mansions see—
I only bow to Nature's God—
The land of shades will do for me.

PHILIP FRENEAU
"THE INDIAN STUDENT"

Archangels on Ice—Wee! You've never seen an ice show like this. Triple lutzes! Quadruple spins! Ten Lords a Leaping! Legions of Snow Angels glide along in the Angelic Ice Parade, with commentary by David Letterman's great-great-grandmother.

ANNIE PIGEON
THE VISITOR'S GUIDE TO THE AFTERLIFE

Shall we gather at the river
    Where bright angel feet have trod;
With its crystal tide forever
    Flowing by the throne of God?

ROBERT LOWRY

The proof if heaven be, or only seem,
That we forever choose what we will dream!

HELEN HUNT JACKSON

Who Are Angels?

In heaven an angel is nobody in particular.

GEORGE BERNARD SHAW

An angel is a spiritual being, created by God, without a body, for the service of Christendom and the Church.

MARTIN LUTHER
TABLE TALK

What know we of the Blest above
But that they sing, and that they love?

WILLIAM WORDSWORTH
"SCENE ON THE LAKE OF BRIENZ"

The superiority of angels increases in proportion as the number of species [concepts] required by them in order to apprehend the universe of intelligibles decreases.

ETIENNE GILSON

The angel personifies something new arising from the deep unconscious.

C. G. JUNG

It is not because angels are holier than men or devils that makes them angels, but because they do not expect holiness from one another, but from God alone.

WILLIAM BLAKE

It is said by some who ought to understand such things, that the good people, or the fairies, are some of the angels who were turned out of heaven, and who landed on their feet in this world, while the rest of their companions, who had more sin to sink them, went down farther to a worse place.

WILLIAM BUTLER YEATS
FAIRY TALES OF IRELAND

That's not just a woman living across your street. That's an angel.

OSSIE DAVIS
AS CHUCK IN DONALD PETRIE'S GRUMPY OLD MEN

[Angels] are not merely forms of extraterrestrial intelligence. They are forms of extra-cosmic intelligence.

MORTIMER J. ADLER
THE ANGELS AND US

An angel is like a good executive secretary.

ANDRE D'ANGELO

*I*t is not impossible to conceive, nor repugnant to reason, that there may be many species of spirits, as much separated and diversified one from another by distinct properties whereof we have no ideas, as the species of sensible things are distinguished one from another by qualities which we know and observe in them.

JOHN LOCKE

*T*here are four large old thunderbirds. The great wakinyan of the west is the first and foremost among them. He is clothed in clouds. His body has no form, but he has huge, four-jointed wings. He has not feet, but he has claws, enormous claws. He has no head, but he has a huge beak with rows of sharp teeth. His color is black. The second thunderbird is red. He has wings with eight joints. The third thunderbird is yellow. The fourth thunderbird is blue. This one has neither eyes nor ears.

LAME DEER

*A*ngels are waves of energy.

CYNTHIA ROSE YOUNG

"*A*re you the conductor?" she asked.
"The conductor of what?"
"The conductor of verisimilitude?"

CHARLES BUKOWSKI
"BRING ME YOUR LOVE"

*T*hey are celestial visitants, flying on spiritual, not material, pinions. Angels are pure thoughts of God, winged with Truth and Love, no matter what their individualism may be.

MARY BAKER EDDY

For in the resurrection they neither marry, nor are given in marriage, but are as the angels of God in heaven.

MATTHEW 23:30

An angel may be any member of the celestial hierarchy, especially of the lower orders. It does not need to wear wings, although this is a fond belief of many Christian and otherwise orthodox artists who can paint feathers better than feet, which are often covered by folds of thick cloth.

M. F. K. FISHER
As They Were

Angels are spirits, but it is not because they are spirits that they are angels. They become angels when they are sent, for the name *angel* refers to their office, not their nature. You ask the name of this nature, it is *spirit*; you ask its office, it is that of an angel, which is a messenger.

ST. AUGUSTINE

The test of a true myth is that each time you return to it, new insights and interpretations arise.

STARHAWK (MIRIAM SIMOS)
THE SPIRAL DANCE

The milky blue angels were infinitely sad. They had travelled a long way. When Eugene was gone they would still travel on and on, until one day no one knew who they were any more. There was only this travelling.

IRIS MURDOCH
THE TIME OF THE ANGELS

Angels–All the people who worshipped God on earth and like meant it get to be angels. That means they get to fly around and play old time guitars and stuff. But what sucks is that only God and Jesus and his like roadies get to have beards and stuff. It's like ZZ Top's family or something.

BEAVIS AND BUTT-HEAD ENSUCKLOPEDIA

That is a Spirit which comes both from above and below.

NATIVE AMERICAN SAYING

Bluebeard: We can easily find out whether she is an angel or not. Let us arrange when she comes that I shall be the Dauphin, and see whether she will find me out.

GEORGE BERNARD SHAW
SAINT JOAN

One of my favorite expressions is "Angels fly because they take themselves lightly." To me, that means they're not held down by the weight of their own self-importance. They don't ever think of themselves as angels. They just are. Angels are very special to me. I'm not for a moment suggesting that I am an angel, but I have certainly known some.

DOLLY PARTON

People see God every day; they just don't recognize him.

PEARL BAILEY

An integral being knows without going, sees without looking, and accomplishes without doing.

LAO TZU

Many a long dispute among divines may be thus abridged: It is so. It is not so. It is so. It is not so.

BENJAMIN FRANKLIN
POOR RICHARD'S ALMANACK

The death of God left the angels in a strange position. They were overtaken suddenly by a fundamental question. One can attempt to imagine the moment. How did they *look* at the instant the question invaded them, flooding the angelic consciousness, taking hold with terrifying force? The question was, "What are angels?"

DONALD BARTHELME
"ON ANGELS"

That's all an angel is, an idea of God.

MEISTER ECKHART

Angels, spirits, demons and the like may feature in dreams either as symbols of blessing or warning or as symbols of parts of yourself which could lead you to greater fulfillment or, if neglected and scorned, could severely damage your chances of happiness.

ERIC ACKROYD
A DICTIONARY OF DREAM SYMBOLS

Guardian Angels

Sleep, my child, and peace attend thee
All through the night;
Guardian angels God will send thee
All through the night.

SIR HAROLD BOULTON

I've heard that little infants converse by smiles and signs
With the guardian band of angels that round about them shines

CAROLINE ANNE SOUTHEY

Lullaby and goodnight,
Thy mother's delight,
Fair angels above
Will guard thee in love;
They will keep thee from harm,
Thou shalt wake in my arms;
They will keep thee from harm,
Thou shalt wake in my arms.

JOHANNES BRAHMS
"LULLABY"

The angels are the dispensers and administers of the divine benefi-
cence toward us, they regard our safety, undertake our defense, direct
our ways, and exercise a constant solicitude that no evil befalls us.

JOHN CALVIN
INSTITUTES OF THE CHRISTIAN RELIGION, VOLUME 1

Curse his better angel from his side,
And fall to reprobation.

WILLIAM SHAKESPEARE
OTHELLO

We are neither the light, nor the message. We are the messengers.
We are . . . nothing. You are . . . for us . . . everything.

WIM WENDERS
FARAWAY, SO CLOSE!

When you are lonely or frightened, talk to your guardian angel.
You can do it out loud or inside your head—your angel can hear you.
Ask your angel to be near you, to put his or her hand on your shoul-
der, to give you courage and protect you.

JOAN WESTER ANDERSON
WHERE ANGELS WALK

There were six or seven pictures: an ugly *Last Supper* in blue and
yellow, a *Guardian Angel* pushing two children along a path at the
edge of a cliff, a study of flowers—

ELIZABETH BISHOP
"GREGORIO VALDES"

A guardian angel o'er his life presiding,
Doubling his pleasures, and his cares dividing.

SAMUEL ROGERS
"HUMAN LIFE"

*A*ngel of God, my guardian dear
To whom God's love commits me here;
Ever this day be at my side,
To light and guard, to rule and guide.

CATHOLIC PRAYER

*T*he question is, why are you saved with your guardian angel and not the woman who was shot to death shielding her children in Brooklyn three weeks ago? That suggests a capricious divine force. If there is a God, he can't possibly work that way.

TONY KUSHNER

*H*e asks no angel's wing, no seraph's fire;
But thinks, admitted to that equal sky,
His faithful dog shall bear him company.

ALEXANDER POPE
"ESSAY ON MAN"

*O*nce a dream did weave a shade
O'er my Angel-guarded bed.

WILLIAM BLAKE
"A DREAM"

A man does not always choose what his guardian angel intends.

ST. THOMAS AQUINAS

George: Well you look about like the kind of an angel I'd get. Sort of a fallen angel, aren't you? What happened to your wings?

Clarence: I haven't got my wings yet, that's why I'm an angel second-class.

FRANK CAPRA
IT'S A WONDERFUL LIFE

"*G*o to her Lewis," said the angel. "Go to her. Return to her life and remind her that materialism is a superficial value. Teach her to cope with loss. Discourage her from being such a damn control freak. Remember, Lewis . . . no dog's life is a failure so long as he still has expensive items to shred."

And so, the angel watched as the big wet dog galumph-galumph-galumphed back to his home.

MERRILL MARKOE
"IT'S A WONDERFUL LEWIS"

I dedicate these pages to my guardian angel, impressing upon him that I'm only fooling and warning him to see to it that there is no misunderstanding when I go home.

FLANN O'BRIEN
THE DALKEY ARCHIVE

James Mason: You know what I am?

Lucille Ball: You mean that guardian angel bit? Oh, is that so. . . . Well, I want to ask you something, Mr. Angel. If you're what you say you are, why do you look like James Mason?

James Mason: I look the way you want me to look.

ALEXANDER HALL
FOREVER DARLING

*W*henever we have to speak with someone who is rather closed to our argument and with whom therefore the conversation needs to be very persuasive, we go to our guardian angel.

POPE PIUS XI

*P*ut your faith in the Lord, and you'll never be alone.

SARAH AND A. ELIZABETH DELANY

*T*ell him a faithful one is doing
  All that love can do
Still that his path may be worth pursuing,
  and to bring peace thereto.

THOMAS HARDY
"THE HAUNTER"

I fly the flight of the fluid and swallowing soul,
My course runs below the soundings of plummets.

I help myself to material and immaterial,
No guard can shut me off, no law can prevent me.

WALT WHITMAN
LEAVES OF GRASS

*E*ven in his lamentations are unheard,
        though now,
in for the long haul, trying to live

beyond despair, he believes, he needs
        to believe
everything he does takes root, hums

beneath the surfaces of the world.

STEPHEN DUNN
"THE GUARDIAN ANGEL"

*M*aybe, you answered, maybe everyone carries a plan inside, but
it's a faded map that's hard to read and that's why we wander
around so and sometimes get lost.

ISABEL ALLENDE
THE INFINITE PLAN

A thanksgiving to spiritual beings assigned to help human beings
carry out their duties.

OREN LYONS
FAITHKEEPER, TURTLE CLAN OF THE ONONDAGA IROQUOIS NATION

*T*he sheen of my sandals is dulled by the dust of cloves. My wings are waxed with nectar. My eyes are diamonds in whose facets red gold is mirrored. My face is a mask of ivory: Love me. Listen to my promises:

JOHN UPDIKE
"ARCHANGEL"

I feel that one must turn to God in faith, knowing that His loving-kindness is never far from us and that His providence never allows us to be tested beyond our strength. If we truly believe in His presence and goodness to us, we are never alone, or forsaken.

ROSE FITZGERALD KENNEDY

*S*he was alone at last. There was not even a ghost left now to drift with through the years. She might stretch out her arms as far as they could reach into the night without fear that they would brush friendly cloth.

F. SCOTT FITZGERALD
NOTEBOOKS

*A*ngel: Greetings, Prophet;
        The Great Work begins:
        The Messenger has arrived.

TONY KUSHNER
ANGELS IN AMERICA, PART I

Cathedral

*G*reat moment; Byzantine angels burn incense.
Love answers again: *Credo*. Ah, here all is love! The organ
seems to throw flowers along the way. What living purity!

AUGUSTE RODIN
ON MASS AT THE CATHEDRAL OF LIMOGES

*T*he Mass is a sacramental participation in the liturgy of heaven,
the cult officially rendered to the Trinity by the full host of the spiritual creation. The presence of the Angels at Mass introduces the
Eucharist into heaven itself.

CARDINAL DANIELOU

I remembered the daily chorus of ninety singers in the little concert-
room at the conservatoire, and seeing that St. Peter's would hold at
least sixty times as many, I came to the conclusion that the choir of
St. Peter's must number some thousands.

There are *eighteen* on ordinary days and *thirty-two* on solemn
festivals! I have even heard a *Miserere* in the Sistene Chapel by *five*
voices.

HECTOR BERLIOZ

*W*herever one perceives a loftier, darker coloration to human endeavors, one may assume that the fear of spirits, the smell of incense, and the shadow of churches have remained attached to them.

FRIEDRICH NIETZSCHE
HUMAN, ALL TOO HUMAN

*S*o, when the saints are assembled, there will be a double Church, one of men and one of angels.

ORIGEN

*W*hen he [the reverend] spoke of the glory of the resurrection, they saw the three women wonder-stricken before the open tomb, at its side the great and ponderous stone rolled away; he recreated for them the angel standing with his sword of petrified fire; in the fervor of his narration, he gave the angel a name, numbered his wings to the count of six, and told what his specific duties were in heaven. He plied the wings of his imagination and floated away as if on a magic carpet.

COUNTEE CULLEN
ONE WAY TO HEAVEN

*S*he came to the village church,
And sat by a pillar alone;
An angel watching an urn
Wept over her, carved in stone.

ALFRED, LORD TENNYSON
MAUD

*O*r the dry whisper of unseen wings,
Bats not angels, in the high roof.

R. S. THOMAS
"IN A COUNTRY CHURCH"

The dealer [in the body and souls of men] gives his blood-stained gold to support the pulpit, and the pulpit, in return, covers his infernal business with the garb of Christianity. Here we have religion and robbery the allies of each other—devils dressed in angels' robes, and hell presenting the semblance of paradise.

FREDERICK DOUGLASS
LIFE OF AN AMERICAN SLAVE

"Sometimes the cathedrals have devils and such carved into the front. Sometimes lords and ladies. Don't ask me why this is," I said.

RAYMOND CARVER
"CATHEDRAL"

The cathedral is full of children and Marist priests who have come together for a traditional Marian celebration. I feel a little out of place in this community. A simple and prayerful tone is set right at the beginning of the celebration. The Gospel of the angel telling Mary that she will be a mother makes my heart leap.

NICOLE GAUSSERON
CATHEDRAL OF SAINT JOHN, LYONS

Am I, at bottom, still that fervent little Spanish Catholic child who chastised herself for loving toys, who forbade herself the enjoyment of sweet foods, who practiced silence, who humiliated her pride, who adored symbols, statues, burning candles, incense, the caress of nuns, organ music, for whom Communion was a great event?

ANAIS NIN

"*I* let things take their course and my love grew into devotion.

She whom I had loved so much was declared venerable. Later she was beatified, and, fifty years after the discovery of her body, she was canonized. I went to Rome myself to be present at the ceremony, which was the most beautiful spectacle I have ever been given to look upon.

With that canonization, my love entered heaven, I was happy as an angel in paradise, and I quickly came back here, filled with the most sublime and strange happiness in the world, to pray at the altar of Saint Adorata . . ."

VOLTAIRE
"SAINT ADORATA"

I am certainly not the first to be struck by the resemblance between what are called obsessive acts in neurotics and those religious observances by means of which the faithful give expression to their piety. The name "ceremonial," which has been given to certain of these obsessive acts, is evidence of this. The resemblance, however, seems to me to be something more than superficial, so that an insight into the origin of neurotic ceremonial may embolden us to draw by analogy inferences about the psychological processes of religious life.

SIGMUND FREUD
CHARACTER AND CULTURE

*O*ne thing is certain: nothing, absolutely nothing, in the philosophic, esthetic, morphological, biological or moral discoveries of our epoch denies religion. On the contrary, the architecture of the temple of special sciences has all its windows open to heaven.

SALVADOR DALI

*T*he *E*thereal and *E*ternity

*E*asier than air with air, if Spirits embrace,
Total they mix, union of pure with pure
Desiring, no restrained conveyance need
As flesh to mix with flesh, or soul with soul.

JOHN MILTON
PARADISE LOST

*H*eaven And Hell Are Just One Breath Away

ANDY WARHOL
TITLE OF HIS LAST WORK

I am thinking of aurochs and angels, the secret of durable pigments, prophetic sonnets, the refuge of art.

VLADIMIR NABOKOV
LOLITA

I go to meet my image and my image comes to meet me: it caresses and embraces me as if I were returning from captivity.

MANDAEAN LITURGY OF THE DEAD

The absolute absence of a burden causes man to be lighter than air, to soar into the heights, take leave of the earth and his earthly being, and become only half real, his movements as free as they are insignificant.

What then shall we choose? Weight or lightness?

MILAN KUNDERA
THE UNBEARABLE LIGHTNESS OF BEING

The greatest form has no shape.

LAO TZU

Spiritus, the divine breathe, inspiration. And now it's your turn to give it back. That's how the whole thing works.

AUDREY HEPBURN
AS THE ANGEL IN STEVEN SPIELBERG'S ALWAYS

Time is man's angel.

JOHANN VON SCHILLER

Praised be all the angels for ever.

TOBIT 11:15

Etherial minstrel! Pilgrim of the sky.

WILLIAM WORDSWORTH

Let us see, is this real,
Let us see, is this real,
This life I am living?
You, Gods, who dwell everywhere,
Let us see, is this real,
This life I am living?

PAWNEE PRAYER

The present is the point of power.

KATE GREEN
NIGHT ANGEL

She with one breath attunes the spheres,
    And also my poor human heart,
With one impulse propels the years
    Around, and gives my throbbing pulse its start.

HENRY DAVID THOREAU
"INSPIRATION"

There are certain works of ours, done indeed out of your gift, but they are not eternal. After such things, we hope to find rest in your great sanctification. But you, the Good, needful of no good, are forever at rest, for your rest is yourself.

What man will give it to a man to understand this? What angel will give it to an angel? What angel to man? From you let it be asked. In you let it be sought. At your door let us knock for it. Thus, thus is it received, thus is it found, thus is it opened to us.

ST. AUGUSTINE
THE CONFESSIONS OF ST. AUGUSTINE

Ethereal, pervading all, (for without me what were all? what
        were God?)
Essense of forms, life of the real identities, permanent,
        positive, (namely the unseen,)
Life of the great round world, the sun and stars, and of man,
        I, the general soul,
Here the Square finishing, the solid, I the most solid,
Breathe my breath also through these songs.

WALT WHITMAN
"CHANTING THE SQUARE DEIFIC"

Whether invoked or not, God will be present.

C. G. JUNG
WORDS OVER THE ENTRYWAY TO HIS HOME

God does not die on the day when we cease to belive in a personal diety, but we die on the day when our lives cease to be illuminated by the steady radiance, renewed daily, of a wonder, the source of which is beyond all reason.

DAG HAMMARSKJOLD

*A*n eldil [angel] is not more needful to Him than a grain of Dust: a peopled world no more needful than a world that is empty: but all needless alike, and what all add to Him is nothing.

C. S. LEWIS
PERELANDRA

*W*hen Siddhartha listened attentively to this river, to this song of a thousand voices; when he did not listen to the sorrow or laughter, when he did not bind his soul to any one particular voice and absorb it in his Self, but heard them all, the whole, the unity; then the great song of a thousand voices consisted of one word: Om—perfection.

HERMANN HESSE
SIDDHARTHA

*W*isdom and Spirit of the universe!
Thou Soul that art the Eternity of Thought!
That giv'st to forms and images a breath
And everlasting motion!

WILLIAM WORDSWORTH
"THE PRELUDE"

*S*tars and blossoming fruit trees: Utter permanence and extreme fragility give an equal sense of eternity.

SIMONE WEIL
GRAVITY AND GRACE

*W*hatever befalls you was prepared for you beforehand from eternity, and the thread of causes was spinning from everlasting both your existence and this which befalls you.

MARCUS AURELIUS

*A*nd, sometimes, horror chills our blood
　　To be so near such mystic Things,
And we wrap round us, for defence,
Our purple manners, moods of sense—
As angels, from the face of God,
　　Stand hidden in their wings.

ELIZABETH BARRETT BROWNING
"A Sabbath Morning at Sea"

*h*i-niswa' vita'ki'ni
We shall live again.

CHEYENNE GHOST DANCE PRAYER

*W*e come spinning out of nothingness, scattering stars like dust.

JALALUDDIN RUMI

Steps unto Heaven

There let the way appear
      Steps unto heaven;
All that thou sendest me
      In mercy given;
Angels to beckon me
Nearer, my God, to thee,
      Nearer to thee!

SARAH F. ADAMS
"NEARER, MY GOD, TO THEE"

And those musicians that shall play to you
Hang in the air a thousand leagues from hence,
And straight they shall be here.

WILLIAM SHAKESPEARE
HENRY IV, PART I

If the archangel now, perilous, from behind the stars took even one step down toward us, our own heart, beating higher and higher, would beat us to death.

RAINER MARIA RILKE

The space between heaven and earth is like a bellows.
The shape changes but not the form;
The more it moves, the more it yields.

LAO TZU

"Pass in, pass in," the angels say,
"In to the upper doors,
Nor count compartments of the floors,
But mount to paradise
By the stairway of surprise."

RALPH WALDO EMERSON

In the woods around her the invisible cricket choruses had struck
up, but what she heard were the voices of the souls climbing upward
into the starry field and shouting hallelujah.

FLANNERY O'CONNOR
REVELATION

The path has been marked. And it will be called Angelwalk,
throughout the totality of eternity.

ROGER ELWOOD

Around our pillows golden ladders rise,
        And up and down the skies,
        With winged sandals shod,
The angels come, and go, the Messengers of God!

RICHARD HENRY STODDARD
"HYMN TO THE BEAUTIFUL"

*A*nd he [Jacob] dreamed, and behold a ladder set up on the earth, and the top of it reached to heaven: and behold the angels of God ascending and descending on it.

GENESIS 28:12

Colored like gold, on which the sunshine gleams,
  A stairway I beheld to such a height
  Uplifted, that mine eye pursued it not.
Likewise beheld I down the steps descending
  So many splendors, that I thought each light
  That in the heaven appears was there diffused.
And as accordant with their natural custom
  The rooks together at the break of day
  Bestir themselves to arm their feathers cold;
Then some of them fly off without return,
  Others come back to where they started from,
  And others, wheeling round, still keep at home.

DANTE ALIGHIERI
PARADISO, CANTO XXI

Angel Food

[Angels are in a way] a seasoning to make God more palatable.

JULIA CHILD

If an angel out of heaven
Brings you other things to drink,
Thank him for his kind attention.
Go and pour them down the sink.

G. K. CHESTERTON
THE SONG OF RIGHT AND WRONG

From that day on he would always think of Perrin—who later came to detest the drink as oversweet, the epitome of his early lack of sophistication, his suburban pretensions—as synonymous with that first occasion, when they had both tremblingly met and Perrin's mode of identification was, along with Edith Sitwell, a long amethyst scarf, a sense of the early Oscar Wilde, and a drink called Fallen Angel.

PETER WELLS

*A*nd as [Elijah] lay and slept under a juniper tree, behold, then an angel touched him, and said unto him, Arise and eat. And he looked, and, behold, there was a cake baken on the coals, and a cruse of water at his head. And he did eat and drink, and laid him down again. And the angel of the Lord came again the second time, and touched him, and said, Arise and eat; because the journey is too great for thee.

I KINGS 19:5–7

Tagliolini–also known as *capelli d'angelo* or angel hair.

MARCELLA HAZAN
ESSENTIALS OF CLASSIC ITALIAN COOKING

*B*lack as the devil,
Hot as hell,
Pure as an angel,
Sweet as love.

CHARLES MAURICE DE TALLEYRAND-PERIGORD
RECIPE FOR COFFEE

A perfect angel food cake is light, puffy, and cloud-like with a
crispy crust.

JULEE ROSSO AND SHEILA LUKINS
THE NEW BASICS COOKBOOK

*S*itting on its pedestal, in a dark purple puree of blackberry, the
Brown Sugar Angel Food Cake attracted lots of attention.

MARTHA STEWART

*W*e had fine weather except for one day, and even this one day
caused us no discomfort as my carriage (I should like to give it a
kiss!) is magnificent. At Ratisbon we dined royally at midday, to the
accompaniment of divine music, with angelic cooking and most
excellent Moselle wine.

WOLFGANG AMADEUS MOZART
IN A LETTER TO HIS WIFE, SEPTEMBER 28, 1790

ORANGE ANGEL TORTE

*M*akes 12 servings

1 cup cake flour
½ cup confectioners' sugar
½ teaspoon salt
Grated zest of 2 oranges
½ cup ground almonds
10 large egg whites
1 teaspoon cream of tartar
¾ cup granulated sugar
1 teaspoon orange extract
Confectioners' sugar, for garnish

1. Preheat oven to 325° degrees F.

2. Sift together the flour, confectioners' sugar, and salt onto a piece of waxed paper. In a large bowl, stir together the flour mixture, orange zest, and almonds.

3. In large bowl, using an electric mixer set on medium speed, beat the egg whites until frothy. Beat in the cream of tartar. Gradually add the granulated sugar and beat at high speed until stiff, but not dry, peaks form.

4. Using a large spatula, gently fold in the orange extract. Slowly and carefully fold the flour mixture into the egg whites, taking care not to deflate them.

5. Turn the batter into an ungreased 10-inch tube pan and smooth the top. Bake until the cake is well-risen, golden brown, and the top springs back when lightly pressed, about 45 minutes.

6. Remove cake from oven and invert the pan onto its raised feet if it has them, or hang the cake around the neck of a heavy glass bottle, or a metal funnel. This will keep the cake from sinking. Let the cake cool completely before serving, then dust with the confectioners' sugar and cut with a serrated knife.

MELISSA CLARK

Angel food cake is a salient example of what can be achieved by
the power of beaten whites.

GOURMET'S BEST DESSERTS

[Chocolate Lover's Angel Food Cake] has many special qualities,
not least of which is that it is the only cake I deem worth eating that
has not even a smidgen of "devil" cholesterol.

ROSE LEVY BERANBAUM
THE CAKE BIBLE

Come Eate thy fill of this thy God's White Loafe?
Its Food too fine for Angells, yet come, take
And Eate thy fill. Is Heavens Sugar Cake.

EDWARD TAYLOR
"MEDITATION: I AM THE LIVING BREAD"

The Angels' Bread is made
The Bread of man today

ST. THOMAS AQUINAS

Hosanna

The angels sing the praise of their Lord and ask forgiveness for
those on earth.

THE KORAN

African Guardian of Souls, Drunk with rum,
Feasting on a strange cassava,
Yielding to new words and a weak palabra
Of a white-faced sardonic god—
Grins, cries
Amen,
Shouts hosanna.

JEAN TOOMER
Cane

Praise God, from whom all blessings flow;
Praise him, all creatures here below;
Praise him above, ye heavenly host;
Praise Father, Son, and Holy Ghost.

EVENING HYMN

I believe in one God, Father Almighty, Maker of heaven and earth, And of all things visible and invisible.

NICENE CREED
325 A.D.

*T*he very thunder speaks His praise and the angels stand in awe of Him. . . . All things in the heavens and the earth bow in worship of God whether of their own volition or volition apart, as do their shadows by morning and evening.

THE KORAN

*G*lories stream from heaven afar
Heav'nly host sing Allelujah

JOSEPH MOHR
"SILENT NIGHT"

The first Noel, the angel did say
Was to certain poor shepherds
In fields as they lay

14TH-CENTURY HYMN

You can rejoice in who you are as a species, born from the heart of God along with the angels. From your heart, out to the world— rejoice!

ANDREW RAMER
ANGEL ANSWERS

Stricken with fear, the two men fell to the ground. But Raphael said to them: No need to fear; you are safe. Thank God now and forever. As for me, when I came to you it was not out of any favor on my part, but because it was God's will. So continue to thank him every day; praise him with song.

THE TOBIT

Give ye praise,
all angels,
to him above
who is worthy of praise.

ZULU PRAYER

"Glory be to the Father, to the Son,
    And Holy Ghost!" all Paradise began,
    So that the melody inebriate made me.

DANTE ALIGHIERI
PARADISO, CANTO XXVII

Lofty Ambition

He returned to the world of the stars and the songs and the night and the ancient wall, grasping at the tail ends of the vision; his fingers sunk into the waves of majestic darkness. He jumped to his feet, drunk on inspiration and power. Don't be sad, his heart told him. One day the door may open to greet those who seize life boldly with the innocence of children and the ambition of angels.

NAGUIB MAHFOUZ
THE HARAFISH

Man can will nothing unless he has first understood that he must count on no one but himself; that he is alone, abandoned on earth in the midst of his infinite responsibilities, without help, with no other aim than the one he sets for himself, with no other destiny than the one he forges for himself on this earth.

JEAN PAUL SARTRE

Here we are. Let us say Yes to our presence in Chaos.

JOHN CAGE
"WHERE ARE YOU GOING? WHAT ARE WE DOING?"

Do not imagine that you must wonder—
only dare to encounter it

PIRKE AVOT

Not like Dante
                    discovering a *commedia*
                                        upon the slopes of heaven
I would paint a different kind
                              of Paradiso
in which the people would be naked
                            as they always are
                                        in scenes like that
                    because it is supposed to be
                                        a painting of their souls
but there would be no anxious angels telling them
            how heaven is
                        the perfect picture of
                                    a monarchy
                and there would be no fires burning
                        in the hellish holes below
                in which I might have stepped
        nor any altars in the sky except
                                    fountains of imagination

LAWRENCE FERLINGHETTI
FROM A CONEY ISLAND OF THE MIND

fling away ambition:
by that sin fell the angels; how can man then,
The image of his Maker, hope to win by't?

WILLIAM SHAKESPEARE
HENRY VIII

Self-knowledge is so important that, even if you were raised right up to the heavens, I should like you never to relax your cultivation of it; so long as we are on this earth, nothing matters to us more than humility. And so I repeat that it is a very good thing—excellent, indeed—to begin by entering the room where humility is acquired rather than by flying off to the other rooms. For that is the way to make progress, and, if we have a safe, level road to walk along, why should we desire wings to fly?

ST. TERESA OF AVILA
INTERIOR CASTLE

The man form is higher than the angel form; of all forms it is the highest. Man is the highest being in creation, because he aspires to freedom.

PARAMAHANSA YOGANANDA

When our two souls stand up erect and strong,
Face to face, silent, drawing nigh and nigher,
Until the lengthening wings break into fire
At either curved point,—what bitter wrong
Can the earth do to us, that we should not long
Be here contented? Think. In mounting higher,
The angels would press on us and aspire
To drop some golden orb of perfect song
Into our deep, dear silence. Let us stay
Rather on earth, Beloved,—where the unfit
Contrarious moods of men recoil away
And isolate pure spirits, and permit
A place to stand and love for a day,
With darkness and the death-hour rounding it.

ELIZABETH BARRETT BROWNING

We want, this fire so burns our brain tissue,
to drown in the abyss—heaven or hell,
who cares? Through the unknown, we'll find the new.

CHARLES BAUDELAIRE
LES FLEURS DU MAL

I asked for a good life—thanking God who gave me life. This I did.
And as the drum was beating, my body shook in time to the beat. I
was unaware of it. I was just very contented. I never knew such pleasure as this. There was a sensation of great joyousness. Now I was an
angel. That is how I saw myself. Because I had wings I was supposed
to fly but I could not quite get my feet off the ground,—I wanted to
fly right away, but I could not because my time is not yet completed.

MOUNTAIN WOLF WOMAN

Through feeble Infancy is steered the Bark of Life
By Angel hands; but growing man demands
The helm in confidence & dares the strife
Of the far-sweeping waves.

THOMAS COLE
"THE VOYAGE OF LIFE, PART SECOND"

The lilting witchery, the unrest
Of winged dreams, is in our breast;
But ever dear Fulfillment's eyes
Gaze otherward. The long-sought prize,
My lute, must to the gods belong.
The dream is lovelier than the song.

JAMES DAVID CORROTHERS

Our demons, our dragons, our dwarfs, our witches and ogres, our
princes and princesses, our kings and queens, our crevices and
grails, our dungeons and our oars are all here now, ready to teach
us. But we have to listen and take them on in the spirit of the heroic
never-ending quest each of us embodies, whether we know it or
not, in the very fabric of a human life lived, for what it means to
be fully human.

JON KABAT-ZINN
WHEREVER YOU GO THERE YOU ARE

We are too late for the gods and too
   early for Being. Being's poem,
   just begun, is man.

MARTIN HEIDEGGER

There are moments when speech is but a mouth pressed
Lightly and humbly against the angel's hand.

JAMES MERRILL
"A DEDICATION"

It is man's high destiny and proof of his immortality too, that his is
the choice between ending the world, effacing it from the long annal
of time and space, and completing it. This is not only his right, but
his privilege too.

WILLIAM FAULKNER

Spirit blows where it wills; enters into fools and inspires them to
do—what they can.

PAUL VALERY

So I beheld more than a thousand splendors
    Drawing towards us, and in each was heard:
    "Lo, this is she who shall increase our love."
And as each one was coming unto us,
    Full of beatitude the shade was seen,
    By the effulgence clear that issued from it.
Think, Reader, if what here is just beginning
    No farther should proceed, how thou wouldst have
    An agonizing need of knowing more.

DANTE ALIGHIERI
PARADISO, CANTO VI

THE END

List of
Illustrations

Aubrey Beardsley
Pages 11,14, 38, 47, 86, 129, 134, 136.

Gustave Dore
Pages 27, 54, 143, 146, 187, 190, from *The Holy Bible;* page 31
from the *Divine Comedy* by Dante Alighieri; pages 58 and 102
from "The Rime of the Ancient Mariner" by Samuel Taylor
Coleridge; and page 124 from *Paradise Lost* by John Milton.

Johann Ulrich Krauss
Page 236, Baroque ornamental cartouche.

William Morris
Page 68, Love and Beauty, allegorical figures from "The
Romaunt of the Rose" by Geoffrey Chaucer in *The Kelmscott
Chaucer.*

Every effort has been made to locate and credit the copyright holders of material quoted in this book. The editor gratefully acknowledges the following for their kind permission to reprint quoted text.

Lines from "The More Loving One" by W. H. Auden, from *W. H. Auden: Collected Poems* by W. H. Auden, edit., E. Mendelson. Copyright © 1976 by Edward Mendelson, William Meredith and Monroe K. Spears, Executors of the Estate of W. H. Auden. Reprinted by permission of Random House, Inc., and Faber and Faber, Ltd.

Lines from "Falling" by James Dickey, from *Poems 1957–1967*. Copyright © 1967 by James Dickey. Reprinted by permission of Wesleyan University Press, University Press of New England.

Lines from #94, #126, and #1544 by Emily Dickinson, from *The Complete Poems of Emily Dickinson*, edit., Thomas H. Johnson. Copyright 1929, 1935 by Martha Dickinson Bianchi; Copyright © renewed 1957, 1963 by Mary L. Hampson. Published by Little, Brown and Company in association with Harvard University Press.

Lines from "Between Angels" and "Guardian Angel" by Stephen Dunn, from *Between Angels*. Copyright © 1989 by Stephen Dunn. Reprinted by permission of W. W. Norton & Co., Inc.

Lines from "A Coney Island of the Mind" by Lawrence Ferlinghetti, from *A Coney Island of the Mind*. Copyright © 1958 by Lawrence Ferlinghetti. Reprinted by permission of New Directions Publishing Corp.

Lines from "Howl" by Allen Ginsberg, from *Collected Poems 1947–1980*. Copyright © 1955 by Allen Ginsberg. Reprinted by permission of HarperCollins Publishers, Inc. and Penguin Books Ltd.

Lines from "Privilege of Being" by Robert Hass, from *Human Wishes*. Copyright © 1989 by Robert Hass. Reprinted by permission of The Ecco Press.

Lines from "Tribute to the Angels" by H.D., from *Collected Poems 1912–1944*. Copyright © 1982 by the Estate of Hilda Doolittle. Reprinted by permission of New Directions Publishing Corp.

Lines from "Pibroch" by Ted Hughes, from *Wodwo*. Copyright © 1961 by Ted Hughes. Reprinted by permission of HarperCollins Publishers, Inc. and Faber and Faber, Ltd.

Lines from "A Dedication" by James Merrill, from *Selected Poems: 1946–1985*. Copyright © 1992 by James Merrill. Reprinted by permission of Alfred A. Knopf, Inc.

Lines from "Men Working on Wings" by Stanley Plumly, from *Boy on the Step*. Copyright © 1989 by Stanley Plumly. Reprinted by permission of The Ecco Press.

Lines from "In the evening your vision widens" by Nelly Sachs, from *O the Chimneys*, translated by Michael Roloff. Copyright © 1967 by Farrar, Straus & Giroux, Inc. Reprinted by permission of Farrar, Straus & Giroux, Inc. and Suhrkamp Verlag.

Lines from "The apple-trees bud, but I do not" by Edna St. Vincent Millay, from *Collected Poems*, HarperCollins. Copyright © 1954, 1982 by Norma Millay Ellis. Reprinted by permission of Elizabeth Barnett, literary executor.

"In the Library" by Charles Simic, from *The Book of Gods and Devils*. Copyright © 1990 by Charles Simic. Reprinted by permission of Harcourt Brace & Co.

Biographical Index

A

Albertus Magnus, 155
    12th- to 13th-century German philosopher; teacher of
    St. Thomas Aquinas
Allen, Woody, 6, 24, 35
    20th-century U.S. filmmaker and writer
Allende, Isabel, 9, 173
    20th-century Chilean novelist
Allston, Washington, 32
    18th- and 19th-century U.S artist and poet
Ambrose, St., 142
    4th-century Italian cleric; Bishop of Milan
Andersen, Hans Christian, 99
    19th-century Danish author; best known for fairy tales
Anderson, Joan Wester, 170
    20th-century U.S. writer
Angelou, Maya, 84
    20th-century U.S. poet; Poet Laureate (1993)
Anthony, Susan B., 95
    19th- and 20th-century U.S. suffragist and editor
Apollinaire, Guillaume, 76
    19th- and 20th-century French poet, art and literary critic
Aquinas, St. Thomas, 51, 94, 171, 193
    13th-century Italian Dominican friar and philosopher
Ardrey, Robert, 114
    19th- and 20th-century U.S. writer
Aristotle, 5, 114
    4th-century B.C. Greek philosopher
Auden, W. H., 121
    20th-century English poet
Augustine, St., 4, 165, 182
    4th- and 5th-century early Christian church father and
    philosopher

B

Bach, Steven, 104
    20th-century U.S. biographer

D

Disraeli, Benjamin, 118
    19th-century British statesman; Prime Minister (1868, 1874-80)
Donne, John, 70, 95, 117
    16th-century and 17th-century English poet, essayist, and cleric
Doolittle, Hilda *See* H.D.
Dostoevsky, Fedor, 6, 84
    19th-century Russian novelist
Douglass, Frederick, 75, 177
    19th-century U.S. journalist and abolitionist
Dryden, John, 94
    17th-century English poet, critic, and playwright; Poet Laureate
    (1668-88)
Dunbar, Paul Laurence, 133
    19th- and 20th-century U.S. poet and novelist
Dunn, Stephen, 44, 173
    20th-century U.S. poet

E

Eadie, Betty J., 60
    20th-century U.S. author
Earhart, Amelia, 78
    19th- and 20th-century U.S. aviator
Eckhart, Meister, 168
    13th- and 14th-century German Dominican theologian
Eddy, Mary Baker, 164
    19th- and 20th-century U.S. writer, theologian; founder of
    Christian Science
Einstein, Albert, 67, 115, 157
    19th- and 20th-century German-born U.S. physicist, originator
    of the theory of relativity; awarded 1921 Nobel Prize for
    Physics
Elliott, Charlotte, 141
    18th- and 19th-century English hymnist
Elwood, Roger, 186
    20th-century U.S. science fiction writer

Freeman, Eileen Elias, 37
    20th-century U.S. writer
Freneau, Philip, 139, 161
    18th- and 19th-century U.S. poet; poet of the American
    Revolution
Freud, Sigmund, 178
    19th- and 20th-century Austrian neurologist; founder of
    psychoanalysis
Fulghum, Robert, 142
    20th-century U.S. writer
Fuller, Margaret, 151
    19th-century U.S. journalist and social reformer

G

Gaffney-Wolfson, Maureen, 39
    20th-century restaurant owner and entertainer
Galland, Adolf, Lieutenant-General, 74
    20th-century German military officer
Gandhi, Mohandas Karamchand (Mahatma), 128
    19th- and 20th-century Hindu spiritual leader and Indian
    nationalist
Garvey, Marcus, 4
    19th- and 20th-century Jamaican black-nationalist leader in the
    United States
Gausseron, Nicole, 177
    20th-century French advocate for the homeless
Geronimo, 46
    19th- and 20th-century Native American Apache chief
Gibran, Kahlil, 23
    19th- and 20th-century Syrian writer and artist
Gilman, Dorothy, 57
    20th-century U.S. writer
Gilson, Etienne, 152, 162
    19th- and 20th-century French philosopher
Ginsberg, Allen, 94
    20th-century U.S. poet

Goebbels, Josef, 97
    19th- and 20th-century Nazi German propaganda director
Goethe, Johann Wolfgang von, 104
    18th- and 19th-century German poet and playwright
Goldberg, Whoopi, 18
    20th-century U.S. actor and comic
Goldman, Karen, 17
    20th-century U.S. writer
Goodbird, Edward, 126
    20th-century Native American writer
Graham, Billy, 5, 29, 95
    20th-century U.S. evangelist and writer
Graham, Martha, 77
    19th- and 20th-century U.S. dancer and choreographer
Grant, Cary, 75
    20th-century U.S. actor
Greeley, Fr. Andrew, 37
    20th-century U.S. cleric, sociologist, and novelist
Green, Kate, 181
    20th-century U.S. poet and writer
Grimes, Karolyn,
    20th-century U.S. actor
Guido, Beatriz, 145
    20th-century Argentinian novelist
Gurganus, Allan, 25
    20th-century U.S. writer

H / I

Haldane, J. B. S., 82
    19th- and 20th-century English geneticist and writer
Hall, Alexander 172
    20th-century U.S. filmmaker
Hammarskjold, Dag, 182
    20th-century Swedish statesman; Secretary General of the
    United Nations (1953-61)
Hanh, Thich Nhat, 93
    20th-century Vietnamese Zen master, poet, and advocate
    for peace

Klee, Paul, 53
  19th- and 20th-century Swiss Abstract painter
Konigsberg, E. L., 45
  20th-century U.S. author of novels for children
Koster, Henry, 75
  20th-century German-born U.S. filmmaker
Kundera, Milan, 180
  20th-century Czech novelist
Kushner, Tony, 37, 56, 65, 171, 174
  20th-century U.S. playwright

L

Lamb, Charles, 122
  18th- and 19th-century English essayist, poet, and literary critic
Lame Deer, 164
  20th-century Sioux medicine man
Lamy, Pere, 86
  19th- and 20th-century French parish priest
Lancaster, Burt, 39
  20th-century U.S. actor
Landon, Lynn, 36
  20th-century U.S. author
Lao Tzu, 152, 167, 180, 186
  6th-century B.C. Chinese philosopher; founder of Taoism
Lawrence, D. H., 113
  19th- and 20th-century English novelist
Laye, Camara, 53
  20th-century U.S. writer
Lennon, John, 131
  20th-century English singer/songwriter
Leonardo da Vinci, 151
  15th- and 16th-century Italian Renaissance artist, writer, and
  inventor
Lewis, C. S., 28, 103, 119, 183
  19th- and 20th-century English scholar and writer
Lincoln, Abraham, 55, 67, 115
  19th-century U.S. statesman; 16th President of the United States

M

Miller, Arthur, 159
    20th-century U.S. playwright
Miller, Henry 95
    19th- and 20th-century U.S. novelist and essayist
Milosz, Czeslaw, 135
    20th-century Polish-born U.S. poet; awarded 1980 Nobel Prize
    for Literature
Milton, John, 33, 63, 104, 109, 123, 128, 130, 179
    17th-century English poet
Mohammed, 133
    6th- and 7th-century Arab prophet; founder of Islam
Mohr, Joseph, 195
    18th- and 19th-century Austrian cleric and poet
Montaigne, Michel de, 5
    16th-century French essayist
Montgomery, James, 93
    18th- and 19th-century British poet
Moody, Raymond, 97
    20th-century U.S. physician and author
Moore, Thomas, 105
    18th- and 19th-century Irish poet
Moore, Thomas, 21, 105
    20th-century U.S. psychotherapist and writer
Morehead, Philip. D., 13
    20th-century U.S. editor and musicologist
Morrison, Toni, 74
    20th-century U.S. novelist and editor; awarded 1993 Nobel
    Prize for Literature
Mother Teresa, 7, 34, 140, 155
    20th-century Yugoslavian missionary in India
Mountain Wolf Woman, 200
    19th-century Winnebago diarist
Mozart, Wolfgang Amadeus, 191
    18th-century Austrian composer
Munro, H. H. *See* Saki
Murdoch, Iris, 166
    20th-century English novelist

N

Nabokov, Vladimir, 179
   19th- and 20th-century Russian-born U.S. novelist, translator,
   and lepidopterist
Newton, Isaac, 155
   17th- and 18th-century English physicist and mathematician
Nichols, John, 134
   18th- and 19th-century English printer and author
Nietzsche, Friedrich, 3, 176
   19th- and 20th-century German philosopher
Nightingale, Florence, 158
   19th- and 20th-century English nurse and philanthropist
Nin, Anais, 178
   20th-century U.S. author
Nuland, Sherwin B., 101
   20th-century U.S. surgeon and writer

O

O'Brien, Flann, 172
   20th-century Irish writer; pseudonym for Brian O'Nolan
O'Connor, Flannery, 78, 147, 186
   20th-century U.S. novelist, short-story writer, and essayist
Omar Khayyam, 23, 106
   11th- and 12th-century Persian poet, mathematician,
   philosopher, and astronomer
Origen, 141, 176
   2nd- and 3rd-century Alexandrian writer and Christian
   theologian
Ovid, 8, 71
   1st-century B.C. and 1st-century A.D. Roman poet
Owl Woman, 83
   19th-century Papago medicine woman

P

Page, Leopold, 69
   20th-century U.S. survivor of the Holocaust

Q

R

Rumi, Jalaluddin, 40, 144, 184
    13th-century Persian Sufi mystic
Rushdie, Salman, 18, 76
    20th-century British novelist

S

Sachs, Nelly, 37
    19th- and 20th-century German poet and playwright; shared
    1966 Nobel Prize for Literature with S. Y. Agnon
Sackville-West, Vita, 89
    19th- and 20th-century English poet and novelist
Sagan, Carl, 138
    20th-century U.S. astronomer and astrophysicist
Saint-Exupery, Antoine de, 22
    20th-century French aviator and writer
St. James, Elaine, 154
    20th-century U.S. writer
Saki (H. H. Munro), 42
    19th- and 20th-century Scottish writer and satirist
Salinger, J. D., 18
    20th-century U.S. novelist and short-story writer
Sartre, Jean Paul, 197
    20th-century French Existentialist philosopher; awarded but
    refused 1964 Nobel Prize for Literature
Satir, Virginia, 79
    20th-century U.S. psychologist
Schiller, Johann von, 181
    18th- and 19th-century German poet, playwright, and critic
Schultes, Richard Evans, 125
    20th-century U.S. ethnobotanist
Schweitzer, Albert, 16
    19th- and 20th-century French philosopher, missionary,
    physician, and musician; awarded 1952 Nobel Prize for
    Peace
Sears, Edmund Hamilton, 12
    19th-century U.S. cleric and hymnist
Seneca, 154
    1st-century Roman philosopher and statesman

T

Woolf, Virginia, 22, 75, 147
    19th- and 20th-century English novelist, essayist, and
    literary critic
Wordsworth, William, 70, 162, 181, 183
    18th- and 19th-century English poet; Poet Laureate (1843-50)

X / Y / Z

Xenophanes, 90
    6th- and 5th-century B.C. Greek philosopher
Yeats, William Butler, 163
    19th- and 20th-century Irish poet and playwright; awarded 1923
    Nobel Prize for Literature
Young, Cynthia Rose, 164
    20th-century U.S. musician
Young, Dr. Edward, 127
    17th- and 18th-century English poet
Zukav, Gary, 21
    20th-century U.S. writer

*I*ndex

Lee Ann Chearney is president and editorial director of Amaranth, an independent book producer. She was formerly managing editor of the award-winning literary magazine, *Antaeus*.

Elizabeth Spires is the author of four collections of poems, most recently, *Wordling*. She teaches at Goucher College and the Writing Seminars at Johns Hopkins.